The Spyglass

A Childhood in Finland & Sweden

by George Makela

The Spyglass: A Childhood in Finland & Sweden
by George Makela

ISBN: 979-821-85282-2-5

Library of Congress Control Number 2024921616

Edited by Carol Makela
Cover art and illustrations by Sofia E. Rosales Makela
Book design by Jill Flores

Published in association with
Village Books and Paper Dreams
1200 11th Street
Bellingham, WA 98225
villagebooks.com

Printed in the United States of America by IngramSpark

Artistic, scientific, and religious propensities . . .
slumber peacefully together in the small child.

— C.G. Jung

Contents

Introduction

My father died quite unexpectedly on August 21, 2005, when he was seventy years old. His manuscript, *The Spyglass*, sat forgotten for over a decade. It was brought up in conversations as a project that "someone should sometime pursue to publication." A family friend delivered a first edit. However, it was not until the summer of 2019 that I picked it up in earnest and began to try and make sense of the story, to put my father's words into an arrangement that could be shared with the world. There was no longer a digital copy to work with, so I set to work typing his story from a spiral-bound hardcopy version. After two months I completed this first step of the process only to discover that my version was inaccessible due to corrupted files. I sent the hard drive away to a data retrieval company, not knowing if I would see it again. Then, Covid put the world on pause and I began to accept that the work was lost in the pandemonium of the plague. However, in the summer of 2021, I received an email informing me that the file had been recovered and, after a payment of $900 (a small fortune as a part-time teacher, supporting my two grown children) I was able to once again access the manuscript. Dad's story rose to consciousness during a graduate course I was taking which focused on intertextuality and how our memories, artmaking, and

1

writing are influenced over generations by rhizomes woven through history and the humanities. I picked up editing once again after earning my master's degree in Depth Psychology and Creativity from Pacifica Graduate Institute. I completed edits on the fifth draft in June and July of 2023, finishing a day before departing on a month-long journey to the Baltic states and eventually, to Finland. Much care was spent organizing sections into chronological order (to the best of my knowledge and intuition) and to retaining my father's voice, while refining his words.

During hours I spent with this manuscript, I recognized a number of themes woven through my father's experiences as a young child which showed up in his adult life. At times he alludes to one or two of these, but generally the writing remains more narrative than introspective. His is a story that tells what happened, but rarely asks, why did it happen? James Hillman argued that the story of a life should ask "why in the sense of what archetypal idea, myth, or person . . . is at work". [1] For this reason, I wish to focus on the ideas that drove him as well as the myths that may have been at play. I invited his story to take root and live inside my imagination. I discovered and retraced the roads that most influenced him, and in turn, influence me as well.

My father's love of nature threads through much of his story – the joy of being barefoot in the summer, collecting wildflowers and arranging them into bouquets, and hearing the song of the nightingale in the Swedish countryside. I am fortunate that he remained close to the natural world in his role of father to me and my sisters. I remember camping trips in the summertime and being woken up at 4:00am so

[1] Hillman, J. (2019). Healing fiction. Spring Publications, Incorporated.

we could "get on the road" to Eastern Washington to fish in our rowboat. We would spend all day on the lake, snacking on sandwiches with fishing pole in hand. On one such trip I caught eight rainbow trout, quite a feat for a seven- or eight-year-old. Wintertime brought trips to the mountains where we would ski for hours. I have a certain fondness for Campbell's Bean with Bacon soup and hot chocolate, each served from a thermos, visibility limited by the steamed-up car windows. We had an unheated swimming pool in our backyard so we would have cold water in which to plunge ourselves between trips to the sauna. Even though my father lived in a 1970s suburban neighborhood and worked for the Boeing Airplane company, he somehow retained a connection to nature.

There is an element of bodily sensuality throughout the story. To discover the freedom of nudity in the open countryside! His descriptions contain so much joy as to nearly resemble a religious experience: "It was a wonderful feeling being here all alone . . . nakedness gave me a feeling of complete freedom . . . enjoying the solitude of nature." Then there is his discovery of female beauty and sensuality, recalled with curiosity and childlike affection. A crush on a slightly older Swedish girl leads to further explorations of nudity and sensuality. I have been told that my father's love of nudity followed him through the years, and he would sometimes surprise friends with a short, unexpected streak at the most unlikely times.

A love of all things mechanical runs through the entirety of this memoir. There are descriptions of train engines, a rural creamery, a construction set, his self-taught, amateur film career, and a descent into a malfunctioning boiler. It is no wonder that he pursued engineering as an adult. While I believe that my father enjoyed his job as an engineer, I feel that his soul's calling was in the work he enjoyed at home. He taught himself carpentry and made kitchen cabinets and furniture. He visited construction sites, then put that learning into action when he constructed an addition to our family home that included a Finnish sauna. I regularly woke up at five or six in the morning on Saturdays and Sundays to the sound of a tablesaw or the hammering of nails. A bit later in life he became interested in cooking and experimented with a variety of culinary adventures – I recall sausage-making using a meat grinder and the intestines of some unfortunate large animal, the venture into soufflés which required copper mixing bowls, and the best Chicken Kiev I've ever tasted. And there were always boiled potatoes with herring and dill as a memory of home.

Throughout his life, my father loved to travel and reveled in adventure. Even as a young boy sent off on a ship in the middle of winter wartime he was still optimistic and overcome with wonder of the world: "the excitement mounted as we sailed out of the south harbor." Heading through the Swedish countryside en route to his new foster family, his "expectations were at an all-time high." However, despite these peaks in emotion, he was only a six-year-old child and understandably experienced alternating states of trepidation. An uncertain future was always just around the corner. Who knows how often my father teetered between anticipation of new events, and fear of the coming unknown.

How much of memory can we trust, and how do our memories shapeshift over time? How much of our recollections are imagination? How many memories do we hold in our very cells of those who have come before us? Like my father, I love to venture into the unknown and have often found myself in strange and sometimes dangerous situations. Yet, like him, I survived these circumstances and was able to skip down the road shortly after, maybe slightly burned but not beaten. How many of his memories are now mine, as I complete the editing process of his memoir and attempt to frame it in a way that makes sense to our history?

As I edited his words, compiled the pages, and composed my thoughts, a question occurred to me: Is my father here with me? Is he listening? Does he hover over my shoulder as I pause on a word, a phrase, a recollection? I don't know how many of the words I put down here are my own, and how many influences are his. What is the power of ancestry to drive recollection? I know so few of the details; a Finnish person speaks sparsely. An immigrant who longs to melt into the stew of American culture speaks even less of their mother country and culture. Part of my father's childhood memoir is enmeshed in trauma as Russian planes bombarded Helsinki and the countryside during the Winter War of 1939-40. When he sat down to record his memories, how did the passage of time – some fifty or sixty years – alter his perceptions? How much did childhood trauma affect his recollections? How many details were filled in by the workings of imagination? That, perhaps, is one task of the reader. To imagine yourself as a child of wartime, of dislocation, of adventure, loneliness and yes, of the unknown.

Prologue

This is an adventure about my life beginning with my earliest recollections, at age four, through the age of twelve. The early years take place in peaceful Finland, just before the Russian invasion of 1939. After moving to Sweden to escape the onslaught of the Russian army, a new adventure begins which spans over the next three years. Once Finland returns to a safe state, the story returns there. The final episode covers the emigration to yet another new world, America. The original version was written out of sequence and not in any chronological order. My goal is to self-publish this book for the enjoyment of my daughters, relatives, and many friends.

To my daughters, who gave me the inspiration to write about the adventures of my early life in Finland and Sweden, and my arrival in America.

Life in Finland

George with his mother, Bertta.

The Beginnings

My earliest memories reach back to a modest apartment on a little street named Malminkatu in Helsinki, Finland. My birth name was Jyrki, but I was often called by my middle name, Matti, after my grandfather. I lived with my mother Bertta and my aunt Sylvi. My mother was apprenticing as a furrier, which is a step up from a seamstress. She had moved to Helsinki in her late teens partly to get away from home and her stern father in Inkeroinen, a small rural town some 140 kilometers from Finland's capital. She was also attracted by the big city sights and sounds. She first worked as a house cleaner for a well-to-do family, but she soon realized that there must be something better. She eventually found that mending clothes and sewing new women's wear was more to her liking and decided to settle on this occupation until something better came along. She was given additional work in the fur coat trade and found working with furs more rewarding. Though sewing linings into fur coats was challenging, she persevered and soon earned a reputation as

11

a dependable, very exacting, and expeditious worker. Little by little under the tutelage of a master furrier, she learned to assemble small fur pelts and fashion coats using patterns offered by the shop. These heavy coats were excellent in combating the extremely cold winters of Finland. She was on her way up in the big city.

My mother's younger sister Sylvi moved to Helsinki a few years later, also to escape her harsh father. She found a job preparing coffee in commercial sized cookers with Fazer's, a fashionable restaurant and coffee shop located in the business district. Fazer's was widely known for making liqueur-filled chocolates, the finest pastries, and heavenly ice cream. The sisters decided to move into a small flat to ease the high rents. Thus, they came to live on Malminkatu.

One day I appeared into the world as a surprise to everyone. I never knew my birth father, and this fact would plague me in my later life. As I grew up and began to grasp the situation, I understood that I simply didn't have a father. As far as I was concerned, he didn't exist. My mother was exceedingly independent and an extremely proud individual. Having left Inkeroinen as a young woman, she was determined to make the best of it. She was happy to have left home and the authoritarian regime of her father.

As a little boy, I went to Inkeroinen to spend the summers with my grandfather Matti, the strict father from whom my mother and Aunt Sylvi had escaped. My mother found it difficult to provide a home for me and since she needed to work, I spent much of my time in daycare centers. But she wasn't satisfied with this arrangement in the summertime and decided to take me to Inkeroinen to live with her father for the entire summer. At that time, Inkeroinen was an industrialized small town that had two large paper mills. Grandfather worked at the older of the two mills as a machinist where he manufactured paper products from pulp.

My mother and Aunt Sylvi had told me repeatedly that my grandfather was a stern man, short on temper, and that he had pretty much controlled his three daughters with his authoritarian manner. No wonder his oldest daughter, Alma, had left home in her late teens and moved to Berkeley, California in America. Having heard these scare stories about my grandfather, I was more than a little frightened when I was brought to live with this harsh man. My mother was quite worried when she delivered me to her father's care. Grandfather didn't take it lightly when he found out that I had been born out of wedlock.

Grandfather was a wiry, hardworking man, a skilled machinist and not a churchgoer. He liked his drinks every now and then, and when under the influence he became melancholy and teary-eyed. He managed to take a liking to me, perhaps if only because I was a boy. He had a little dog named Seppo, distantly related to a Finnish Spitz, though mostly he was a mutt. He was friendly, always wagging his corkscrew-shaped tail. I took a liking to Seppo, and we became inseparable.

Before my mother returned to Helsinki, she made me promise over and over to not go near the swift-moving river behind the house, and to be extremely watchful of the factory train that ran by the front yard. The train, running on a narrow track, carried sawdust to the old pulp mill, and sometimes machinery and other equipment. Grandfather's home faced the new sawmill across a large grassy field. Its small smokestack, made of red bricks, seemed to scrape the sky, billowing white puffy smoke in the direction of the prevailing wind.

Grandfather worked at the old mill's machine shop six days a week. Sundays were for rest and quiet time. He was always grimy, and his hands were rough and calloused. He left his dirty coveralls at the machine shop, but his clothes smelled of sweat and dirt. Daily bathing was limited to washing oneself using a water-filled pan and soap made from animal fats and lye. Baths were left for Saturday evening in the sauna. Every home had a sauna, some quite crude but nevertheless very efficient. These became weekend rituals to clean the body and refresh the mind. The sauna was heated early in the afternoon by a wood-fired stove. A large built-in metal tank within the stove contained water drawn from the river. The boiling water was mixed with cold water drawn from another tank to suit the bather. Women went first followed by the men and boys. The nearby river offered plenty of cold water for rinsing. Bedtime came much later since it remained light until eleven o'clock in the summertime.

Grandfather smoked a pipe in the evenings. He grew his own tobacco, dried the leaves in the attic, cut the dried leaves and stored them in large humidors. The heavy smoke drifting through the living room left a permanent blue hue. He would sit in the old rocking chair, open the newspaper, and read until he fell asleep. He always farted while sitting in his rocker and the cushions reeked of old farts, which I discovered when I once ventured to smell them. Grandfather was a man of few words, and I feared him silently from a safe distance.

Twice a week he would take me fishing. We always walked along the railroad tracks, crossing several meadows with grazing cows, then upriver where he kept his rowboat tied to the shore near hundreds of lily pads. I gladly accompanied him dressed in just my shorts, barefooted with callused feet. Prancing through the meadows I would step in fresh cow pies, allowing the oozing poop to squish through my toes. More times than not they were still warm and fresh. Grandfather would make me rinse my feet in the river before getting into the rowboat and before going home. Once in the boat we drifted slowly downstream. He had several traps set in the river and would pull them up one by one and empty the trapped fish into the bottom of the boat. We would bring back perch, bass, pike and bream. Occasionally an eel would find its way into the net. The river provided many meals for us; baked fish, fried fish, fish soups, poached fish, and smoked fish kept us alive. Potatoes, beets, rutabaga, and carrots completed the dinner menu.

The factory train chugged by our house several times a day. The engineer would always wave and smile from the cabin window as his train passed by. One day while he switched cars to adjacent tracks, I asked if I could ride with him in the locomotive. To my surprise he gladly lifted me onboard and we rode between the two mills all day long. He stoked the fire with coal and wood chips, pulled the levers and turned the faucets this way and that. He even let me pull the cord to make the train whistle. The chugging sound of the locomotive was music to my ears; the smell of smoke and steam caused my heart to beat loudly. I was in seventh heaven and fascinated with all the machinery. It was the best day of my young life.

Unknown to me, Grandfather had come home a little early and when he couldn't find me to go fishing, called the neighbors to look for me. They searched and called my name to no avail and must have thought that I had surely drowned in the river. In the meantime, I was enjoying myself in the locomotive with the friendly engineer. Back and forth we rode! Finally, the train stopped in front of our house, and I was lifted onto the ground. I wondered why there were so many people milling around until I realized that they had been looking for me. Grandfather came running and when he found me safe, took me into his arms and hugged and squeezed me hard, all the while bawling me out for the trouble I had caused. This stern man held his temper and told me to never, ever take off on my own without telling someone. Having won his blessing, I stayed close to him from then on.

Moving Again

George on city street.

One day Grandfather had a bad accident at the machine shop which broke his left leg in three places. He had slipped on the oily floor and been struck by the large planer.[2] He was put onto a shop truck and taken to a hospital in the nearby city of Kotka. The doctors pinned his leg in several places and put him in traction. He would remain there for several weeks. Luckily my Aunt Sylvi came to Inkeroinen to look after me during Grandfather's hospital stay. I was so glad to see her as she was my absolute favorite aunt. Sylvi, who was single with no children of her own, just adored me. In fact, she had given me her pet name, sametti poski, meaning "velvet cheek." Whenever she hugged me, which

[2] A woodworking machine used to trim boards to a consistent thickness throughout their length.

was every time she saw me, she would tell me how velvety-soft my cheeks were. This pet name would stay with me until I became an adult.

Aunt Sylvi came to Inkeroinen, and we took the train to Kotka to visit grandfather at the hospital. It was a seaport town with many docks and ships. I wished we could have visited the waterfront and spent more time there, but we had come to see Grandfather. We found him in his room with his leg high in the air, held there by cables and pulleys, and weights hanging at the end of the bed. He was concerned about who would look after me. So, what to do? He suggested that Sylvi take me to the home of his elderly Aunt Maiju who lived in Myllykoski, a town close to Inkeroinen. It was agreed that I would stay with Maiju until grandfather was better and could be released from the hospital in Kotka. This was going to be another adventure. Aunt Sylvi stayed with Maiju long enough for me to get to know her a little and once I was settled in, Sylvi returned to Helsinki and her job at Fazer's.

Maiju was hard of hearing and didn't have a hearing aid; not in Finland in 1939. She did possess a curved horn that she used when talking with people. However, half of the time she couldn't find it. If you yelled loudly, she could hear a little and would ad lib the rest. Maiju was a kind woman who took a liking to me, and it seemed that everything would work out alright. Well, almost alright.

Maiju lived on a small farm where she had a little barn, a field of hay and many chickens. Her home was extremely small and consisted of two tiny rooms with plank floors and homemade scatter rugs. The furnishings included modest tables, a couple of chairs, and nothing else. Maiju had very little money, just barely eking out a living off the land. I helped her feed the chickens by sprinkling grain on the ground. The chickens were free to roam around the yard. They laid eggs – small ones, big ones, and once in a while, brown ones. Maiju always got a little milk from one of her neighbors who owned a couple of cows. They hadn't heard of pasteurization in this little community, and I often got to drink milk straight from the cow. One day I learned how to milk one of the cows. At first it was difficult but with a little practice it became easier.

Maiju cooked some rather bland meals. She loved to cook oatmeal mush and vegetable soup. At least she didn't cook fish, thank God for that. She had a strange smell about her which I didn't like – an old woman's smell, of one who doesn't bathe or wash herself well. Partly because of this, I would sneak out into the barn and make a bed out of a pile of straw with an old blanket thrown on top. Eventually I slept out there every night. To my benefit, Maiju was so forgetful that most of the time she didn't miss me when I wasn't around. I began to like the smell of old straw, which was an improvement from the house, and the chickens were no bother.

I spent several weeks there in Myllykoski while grandfather was recovering in the hospital. At last Aunt Sylvi returned to pick me up. Having come late in the afternoon, she was going to spend the night before our departure the following day. I talked her into sleeping in the barn and soon we were tucked away in the straw. We were sound asleep when a thunderous crash woke us up. A spectacular thunderstorm was moving through the area with bolts of lightning illuminating the countryside. The barn roof wasn't waterproofed and drops of rain dripped onto our straw bed. Aunt Sylvi was scared out of her wits, and she hugged me with all her might for comfort and protection. I felt pretty big, not being afraid of a little thunder and lightning. Of course, Maiju slept soundly through the storm. Sylvi couldn't wait to tell Maiju about her terrifying night and she ran into the house the next morning to wake her up. For fifteen minutes she complained about the awful night, how she got all wet in the barn and how the bugs had bitten her all over. Maiju was totally unruffled and kept smiling her toothless smile through Sylvi's story. She didn't care, she didn't hear a thing. Having misplaced her hearing horn seemed a blessing. I couldn't help but laugh over Sylvi's woeful story.

We walked to the train station and boarded the train to Inkeroinen. My grandfather was back from the hospital and learning to walk on crutches. He was not very happy until he got to see me once again. He no longer scared me; he was always good to me. When his leg healed, enabling him to walk again, he resumed working at the mill. In his spare time, he built me a locomotive in the machine shop. It was a small replica of the train that ran between the two mills. I played with this train, sometimes for days on end. When I returned to Helsinki, I brought it back with me. Sadly, somewhere along the way it was lost during a move, and I never saw it again. I wish that I could have kept it as it was such a masterpiece. My grandfather was very gifted and started many home projects which he didn't always finish. Once he began building an upright pump organ. He loved music and he could play expertly even though he couldn't always reach the correct keys having severed two fingertips from his left hand due to a shop accident.

The Winter War

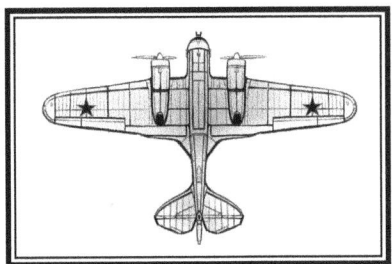

At the end of summer Mother came to bring me back to the city. She had found a preschool for me which was to her liking. Autumn came and it wouldn't be long before the cold, dark winter was here. Then the war started, and the Russians invaded Finland. There was a flurry of activity in the city. All the young men were drafted into the army and sent to the front lines to fight the Russians. Women took over the jobs formerly done by men. They drove trucks, operated streetcars, kept the city clean, ran the food stores, the clothing stores, and all the rest. Large sirens, placed on the rooftops, were readied in case of an attack on the city. It wasn't long before they were wailing with their ear-splitting noise. We were instructed to drop everything and run for the nearest bomb shelter. The shelters were clearly marked on all the city buildings. The Russian planes came in hordes and dropped their deadly payloads upon the city. Some of our friends were killed in the bombings. My mother decided right then and there to send me back to

Inkeroinen to my grandfather's place for safekeeping. As the bombing attacks steadily increased, the city of Helsinki proved to be a most dangerous place. So, off to Inkeroinen I went once again.

There had been much snowfall, and the winter was extremely cold. Grandfather continued his work at the machine shop where they were busy retooling to build war materials, ammunition, and assorted weapons to be shipped to the front lines to confront the approaching enemies. Inkeroinen was no longer a safe haven, as mother had so fervently hoped. The war was extending inland to areas known to have strategic factories, which put this little town firmly on the map. Instead of howling sirens the factories resorted to their loud whistles with intermittent toots to signify an impending attack, and a continuous toot for "all clear."

Grandfather had a sister named Hanna who lived in the same home but on the far side of the house. She was a spinster, though not necessarily by choice, and she was seemingly religious and pious. She always wore a black dress, black stockings and black shoes, and a golden cross necklace, and she had her grayish hair combed straight back, terminating in a bun. No makeup adorned her face, nor a smile. She liked cats, tolerated dogs, and took an instant dislike to me. I disliked her from day one.

Hanna fixed a huge pot of coffee every morning. Grandpa and I would soak stale pieces of bread in the black coffee and eat it with slurping sounds. She packed his lunch box and filled a glass bottle with the hot coffee. Every now and then the bottle would break due to the heat and spill all over the kitchen floor. Thermos bottles didn't exist in the late '30s Finnish countryside. Our pious little lady in black would spout out expletives only used by sailors. Her normally pale face would flush with anger. She didn't relish looking out for her brother and on one of these mornings I had a premonition that my day would not be a good one. She had a way of taking out her own frustrations in the most terrible ways, like the day she decided to go to the neighbor's house for a few minutes and leave me with Seppo and her cat, Ruusu. Hanna had forgotten or maybe purposely chosen not to feed me that morning. As my little tummy began to growl from hunger, I looked for something to eat. She had left cheese remnants in Seppo's dish and what he didn't want I gladly wolfed down to ease the hunger pangs. While I munched on the leftovers meant for Seppo, Hanna suddenly returned home and caught me in the act. Angrily she grabbed a wet dish rag and whipped it against my face. Oh, how that stung! The dishrag spun around my head and snapped against my cheek. She followed up with derisive language, picked up her dear furry Ruusu and departed back to her own quarters. She left me there crying in pain, still hungry, waiting for Grandfather to come home. When he asked how I had gotten the red welt on my cheek I was too frightened to tell him. Hanna was glaring at me from the kitchen, and I knew better than to provoke her any further. Her hate for me was confirmed on that bitter day.

One snowy morning about three weeks after my arrival in Inkeroinen we suddenly heard that dreaded intermittent toot. Hanna, already dressed for the cold morning, hurriedly bundled me up in my white sheepskin winter coat that Mother had made especially for me, and we began our hurried flight across the open field to the bomb shelter.

The mill had blasted a cavern into this massive granite hill to serve as the community shelter. It was crude but nonetheless functional. Heavy steel doors protected the opening. The shelter extended far inside the hill and provided adequate protection for its occupants. Fortunately, Grandfather's home was within walking distance from safety, or so we had thought.

This was the immediate destination for Hanna as she dragged me along in the freshly fallen deep snow. Dozens of neighbors took to the snowy meadow. The deep snow made it extremely difficult to maneuver across this divide. Suddenly several Russian fighter planes appeared from the horizon and began their deadly spray of machine gun bullets and small concussion bombs, their apparent target the multitude of residents and the new paper factory. As the sound of the approaching planes grew louder, Hanna panicked and let go of my hand, leaving me alone in the snow. I heard a whistling sound; unlike any sound I'd heard before. The deep snow had stopped me from making any headway toward the shelter. It was dreamlike, trying to run and not getting anywhere. The whistling suddenly stopped with a muffled thud, followed by an explosion. The shock wave knocked us down as if a giant fist had struck. Suddenly snow, mud, rocks, and shrapnel rained over our heads. The once beautiful white meadow transformed into a nightmarish scene. People were scattered everywhere, some injured and bleeding, adding a terrible red hue to the once pristine snowy meadow.

Hanna was nowhere in sight. Suddenly two young neighbor women approached, risking their lives to pick me up and carry me into the bomb shelter. Four men rushed through the steel doors carrying a litter with an injured man. I stared at this unbelievable sight. The man's intestines were trailing on the ground. Mercifully unconscious, the man had no idea of his fate. The dead were left to lie in the open field to be tended to once the all-clear signal was sounded. There were people everywhere in the crowded shelter. My rescuers asked me how I had gotten there, and I told them that Hanna had run off and left me by myself. They continued to comfort me, and I finally stopped sobbing and shaking. Hanna was found deep in the shelter, unhurt, but extremely troubled, kneeling on the hard ground, praying and sobbing. She couldn't remember abandoning me in the snow, and I still wonder what might have been going on in her head. But at that moment, I hated her. To this day I can clearly recall this traumatic incident.

Many days of the winter of 1940-41 were spent in this remarkable shelter and numerous lives were saved because of it. The shelter is still intact and remains a permanent monument to the war days gone by. I was to see it again years later when I shared memories of my experiences there with my wife and young daughters.

My mother returned to Inkeroinen to collect me and bring me back to Helsinki. It seemed that no place was safe. She felt that I would still be safer in the city even though it was under constant attack. And I would be far away from Hanna. There were more bomb shelters than ever throughout the city and the early warning systems gave ample time in which to seek shelter.

The Russians continued their fierce bombing of Helsinki. We particularly feared cloudless nights during the snowy winters when the moon illuminated the city, clearly revealing the targets to the enemy. Helsinki was totally dark, and woe be to the individual not heeding the mandatory blackouts. As the attacks continued, many people grew nonchalant upon hearing the wailing sirens. Their fear, however, rose to fever pitch when the anti-aircraft guns began to chatter. Hurriedly they fled to the shelters knowing full well that advancing enemy bombers were closing in on their neighborhood. Our bomb shelter was built two floors underground in the hopes that a direct hit would not penetrate it. We were directed to these life-saving shelters quite often. Many nights were spent in these sparse surroundings, in which three-tier bunks were provided for children and the elderly. Communication was available with the aid of a short-wave radio. Sadly, we heard continuing reports of damage inflicted upon the city. "The main post office suffered a direct hit!" . . . "The Helsinki railroad station was destroyed by an incendiary bomb!" . . . "A large, devastating blast leveled three multi-story living quarters in the eastern sector of Helsinki!" On and on the radio kept us in the know of the latest tragic hits.

One night, after spending some seven hours huddled in this crowded, stuffy shelter, a devastating hit on our building caused several bunks to come tumbling down. The entire building shook and rolled in all directions. The lights went out until emergency lighting was established. Cement dust permeated the air and ceiling particles showered the room. Screams and anxious yells were heard throughout the shelter. We were scared out of our wits. The worst thoughts came to mind: Is this the end? Have the gas mains been damaged? Finally, after an interminable wait, the "all clear" signal came. We scurried from the shelter like so many mice to witness the damage. Part of the building's exterior was destroyed, and the rest of the walls were pockmarked with shrapnel damage. Windows were blown out everywhere. Fortunately, the bomb landed a "safe" distance from our building and fell into a clearing. A direct hit would have been fatal. The air was filled with smoke, and the horizon was crimson from burning buildings in the distance. The Russians had flown squadrons of bombers that night. The Finnish military forces were miniscule by any comparison. Our air force had a few planes in their inventory but offered no counterforce to the might of the Russian forces.

Despite the damage caused to the city of Helsinki, I recall a humorous incident celebrated by the entire city. The Russians had dropped an enormous bomb directly on their own five-story embassy building. Rejoice, rejoice! The incendiary bomb destroyed the entire structure. The fire department remained nearby preventing the fire from spreading to adjacent buildings. For three full days the embassy burned and smoldered. Mother and I took a streetcar there to witness this spectacle. Hundreds of people were dancing in the streets. The inside of the building was gutted, though an occasional fireplace or a toilet tank was still visible. What a magnificent memorial. When we departed for America in 1947 the Russian embassy ruins were still there, a commemorative to the winter war.

Escape
to Sweden

[3]

My mother was concerned about my safety. There was talk of sending children to Sweden for their temporary safekeeping. The people of Sweden ended up caring for some seventy to eighty thousand Finnish kids between 1941 and 1944. Sweden remained entirely neutral throughout World War II and would be a godsend to thousands of children. With the help of my mother's friends, arrangements were made to ship me there. I didn't have a vote. I was six years old, about to be sent to a foreign country for an indefinite time, to live with people whom I'd never met and who spoke a language unknown to me.

Sadly, I said goodbye to my friends and to my teary-eyed mother and Aunt Sylvi. Armed with warm clothes and a fistful of labels hanging around my neck, like address labels on a suitcase, I was taken to the south port in Helsinki and placed on board the Swedish vessel SS *Brynhild* along with a host of other apprehensive children and unceremoniously shipped away from the land of my birth.

[3] Brynhild 1953 003, Sjohistoriska museet, Sweden.
  https://picryl.com/media/ss-brynhild 1953-003-710c68

The passengers consisted of hundreds of Finnish boys and girls ranging in age from four to ten. There were many chaperones aboard to assist with this precious cargo. We were escorted to our quarters, four to a cabin with two lower bunks and two up above. I managed to get the lower one, thank you very much. The excitement mounted as we sailed out of the south harbor, following a rugged ice breaker ship. Normal cruise time during the summers was close to fifteen hours. However, this being winter, it became clear that it would take a lot longer for this crossing.

Fear of being discovered by a German U-boat was dangerously real. A thick fog had settled in, making the crossing more difficult on the one hand but safer from being seen by a submarine on the other. The weather was frigid, and the opened channel soon filled with blocks of broken ice. The ship was beginning to pitch up and down, leaving hollow spots in our tummies. The warm cabins were reassuring, and the food made us forget our sadness. I can't remember ever eating such good food. The bread alone must have come from heaven, not to mention the rich butter. I wished that Mother could have been there to enjoy our feast.

While living at home I usually went to bed with my stomach growling from hunger. We never seemed to have enough to eat to satisfy that empty feeling. Sometimes Mother would fix one of my favorite dishes, fried potatoes and onions in pork fat, which emanated a wonderful aroma. Most of the time we ate salted herring and boiled potatoes. Occasionally I brought home a turnip taken from the neighbor's vegetable garden in the darkness of night. This served as a dessert of sorts. Mother was angry when she found how I acquired it, but without saying so she looked the other way. I took this as license to go for more turnips on other nights.

We had entered the Gulf of Bothnia, the body of water separating Finland and Sweden. The temperature kept dropping and the ice was becoming a major problem. The ship slowed to a crawl and before long it came to a stop, unable to continue its movement through the rapidly freezing channel. We became stuck in the ice. The icebreaker had developed mechanical problems, leaving us stranded in the middle of the gulf. We kids were unaware of our predicament since our chaperones kept us busy by having us sing and play all sorts of games to maintain our morale. The ship's engines continued to operate, providing the much-needed comfort levels. We could hardly tell that we weren't moving. The next morning the weather cleared, revealing a white landscape surrounding our ship. We were in winter wonderland. Luckily, another ice breaker had been dispersed from Stockholm to come to our rescue. It arrived at last to reopen the shipping lane, making it possible for us to reach our destination. We kids hadn't the slightest knowledge of the potential danger of being crushed by the ever-growing ice.

At last, the SS *Brynhild* struggled into port in Stockholm. The ship's crew was relieved to reach land and the children were awed by the sight of this large city. We were transported to a nearby hospital which would be the first staging point. Some children who had fallen ill received immediate medical attention. I didn't like hospitals because they always smelled so medicinal. The nurses, dressed in their light blue dresses and white aprons, frightened me. Their nurse's caps were starched and stiff, and we couldn't understand a word they said. We were ushered into a large ward with beds lining both sides of the room, where the doctors examined us one at a time. Inoculations followed. Some kids became feverish following the shots and ended up staying there longer. I managed to remain healthy and waited for the next step in this odyssey.

The day finally came to leave the hospital. Several of us were brought to a nearby hotel where we remained until our final destinations were determined. Some of our ID tags were removed and others added. I felt like an oversized suitcase in a baggage room. I had fun looking out the windows as the streetcars, different from the ones at home, ran back and forth on the busy street below. The snowplows cleared the streets, and cars moved busily to their destinations. I noticed that all the traffic moved on the left side of the street unlike that in Helsinki. Our chaperones kept us busy with interesting new toys during our waiting period. A few days slid by and finally, after saying goodbye to my new friends, I left the hotel with my chaperone and boarded an electric train heading south. The falling snow made the country dreamlike, and my excitement and expectations were at an all-time high. Where was I going? Was I going to live in a city or in the country? Who was I going to live with? Endless questions lingered in my mind. I thought of my mother, living all alone in Helsinki. I wondered what my Aunt Sylvi was doing; was she missing her "velvet cheeks?" I also wondered about my grandfather in Inkeroinen. How was he doing and was he safe at the mill? I felt incredibly lonesome in that moment. I missed being home and I missed my mother. The clickety-clack of the electric train and the landscape speeding by the window were all I had. The future was uncertain and a little scary.

The train came to a stop and my chaperone ushered me into the train station. I was excited and ready to meet my new family. Instead, I was told to sit on a hard wooden bench for some time before boarding yet another train, this time pulled by a steam locomotive. I guess we hadn't yet arrived at the destination. When was this trip going to end? Although I was only six years old, I felt that everything was moving at such a slow pace. The waiting and anticipation were as wearing as the chug-chug-chug of the engine. Whiffs of smoke filled the cabin. This train was much slower than the electric train from Stockholm. Daylight was waning and darkness crept in, leaving the night black except for the snowy landscape. I didn't know what to expect. Lonely and frightened, I sat there looking out into the night. My tummy filled with butterflies, and I was fervently waiting for this long trip to come to an end. I was exhausted and finally fell asleep but was suddenly awakened when the train began to slow. Could this be it? My chaperone gathered my little suitcase and helped me into my winter coat, which my mother had made for me. We stepped down the stairs onto the station platform.

A New Life in Sweden

Ryningsnäs

I arrived at my final destination on a late evening in January 1941. Ryningsnäs was a little farming community in the province of Småland, little more than a whistlestop in the southern region of Sweden.[4] There was a general store next to the railroad station, which also served as the post office. The surrounding landscape was mostly flat, ideal for farming and raising dairy cattle and horses. Most of the land was independently owned by small farmers with the exception of a large farming community governed by a wealthy landowner, or *agronomer*. It was to this community that I had been sent to live with foster parents during the ongoing hostilities in Finland.

My chaperone introduced me to David and Sigrid Persson, who had anxiously been awaiting my arrival. It was frigidly cold, and the landscape was lit by a bright full moon. My traveling companion re-boarded the train and it slowly moved away from the station house. My foster parents smiled gently and spoke to me excitedly with foreign words as I was ushered to their sleigh. The sleigh

[4] The name Småland literally means Small Lands.

horse breathed white vapors which billowed into the cold night air. The night sky was crystal clear, dotted with thousands and thousands of stars. David, or Pelle as he was fondly known, led me to the sleigh and drew back the heavy, fur-lined blankets uncovering a leather bench seat. Sigrid climbed in first and lifted me next to her. Pelle unhitched the horse and turned him around to face the narrow road, then climbed into the sleigh next to me. When the covers were pulled up to my ears, he grabbed the reins and spoke to the horse. The animal started to move in a slow trot as if understanding that strange language. Soon we were traveling on the main road to their home. The snow was packed solidly, and one could hear it creaking under the sleigh's weight. The full moon illuminated the landscape and made it glitter as if covered with a blanket of sparkling diamonds.

As we traveled toward the farm, bells attached to the horse's harness jingled merrily in the cold night. There was magic in the air. I was so excited by the dreamlike atmosphere. No words were spoken during the ride. I didn't know what to expect next, as I had left my home in Helsinki less than two weeks ago and much had happened in that short span of time. As we arrived home to a white, two-story house, Sigrid climbed out of the sleigh with me in tow while Pelle unhitched the horse and led him to the barn. We climbed a narrow flight of stairs to their tiny living quarters where a wood-burning kitchen stove provided heat to both rooms. A bare light bulb hanging from the center of the kitchen ceiling lit up the room, revealing a wooden bench sofa, a small table with two chairs, a narrow sink top and a stand equipped with a pail of drinking water. The adjoining room had a large single bed, a desk and chair, a smaller sized child's bed and a clothes closet. My bed was ready for me and since I was so exhausted, it didn't take long before I was sound asleep.

I woke up the next morning to find Pelle and Sigrid gone. I was alone and wondered where they were. Sigrid returned after a little while and cooked a pot of coffee. She offered me some breakfast and spoke to me excitedly, though I couldn't understand a word she was saying. After dressing me in warm clothing, she took me downstairs to show me where she and Pelle worked. The downstairs of this building contained a dairy creamery, where I saw Pelle busily working with machinery. It dawned on me why they weren't upstairs with me, as the tile floors were wet with water and milk. The machines hummed as Sigrid showed me how the raw milk, delivered to the creamery by horse and sleigh, was dumped into a large collection basin and then pumped to the pasteurizer, the cream separator, and other strange machines. Their workday began at four in the morning and ended around two in the afternoon. They would both take brief naps until the early evening, when dinner was served around six.

As my first days passed in this new country, I began to pick up a new Swedish word here and there. Sigrid was helpful and patient with me, pointing to objects and calling out names. I found that I could speak enough Swedish to be understood and it didn't take long before I could carry on a conversation with *Tant* (Aunt) Sigrid and *Farbror* (Uncle) Pelle, as they preferred to be called. I learned that the Perssons had a daughter who had died of leukemia at the age of twelve. They had mourned her for some time and when the opportunity came to temporarily adopt a child from Finland they jumped at the chance. I was the lucky one to be included in their family.

It didn't take long for me to fully enjoy the treats of the dairy. The fresh, whole milk and all the meals were delicious. Uncle Pelle took me on a long tour of the creamery, and I was fascinated by the cream separator. The whole milk was pumped into one end of this contraption and a heavy, rich cream came pouring out the other end. A taste of this cream with a little added sugar was the nectar of the gods. Each day, Uncle Pelle showed me more features of the creamery. He was enormously proud of his work. He promised that he would show me how butter was churned and how to make cheese and yogurt. Without realizing it, I had stopped thinking about my home in Finland.

Uncle Pelle and Aunt Sigrid got up early each morning and I usually woke up as well since my bed was in the same room. Pelle always paraded around in the nude. He seemed tall to me, with jet black hair, and he was keen to show me everything around the house, perhaps so I would learn to speak better Swedish. It seemed to work. Sometimes he would go to extremes with his demonstrations, stopping in front of my bed to show me numerous scars on his naked abdomen, most likely obtained from past operations. It seemed that he did this repeatedly, as I had already seen them several times. Aunt Sigrid muttered words under her breath, more than likely concerned about my thoughts regarding her husband's actions. One day while he pointed to a particular scar, I couldn't avoid looking at his dangling penis. I reached out with both hands and gave it a hefty tug. This totally unexpected yank surprised him beyond words. He quickly freed himself with embarrassment, skipped across the room, and even more quickly donned his underpants. Aunt Sigrid, standing across the room, burst out laughing until tears streamed from her eyes. Uncle Pelle never showed me his scars again.

# Necessities

Our outhouse was the source of many humorous stories. It had been erected some distance from our home and proved to be quite a walk during the night. In Finland we had indoor plumbing with flush toilets, so it took some time to get used to these outdoor establishments. We had a two-holer, separated by a wall. The left side was shaped with a small hole suitable for women and children, while the other was fitted with a larger aperture, appropriate for men and more generously built people. Toilet paper was unheard of on the farm, so newspapers and catalogs provided the necessary means for cleanup. Old newspapers worked reasonably well except for lingering newsprint adhering to the buttocks. Catalogs weren't quite as good, being slick and lacking that mildly abrasive texture necessary for a clean swipe. The lack of washing facilities necessitated longer use of our underclothes, and careless cleanup was evidenced by tell-tale markings. Filtered lighting peeked through a slatted opening in the door. The lack of electric lighting at nighttime required doing things strictly by feel.

Our outhouse lacked the traditional pit. Instead, two large wooden buckets were strategically positioned in the drop zone. Each bucket had a pair of sturdy handles so that two strapping farm hands could haul them out periodically and replace them with emptied ones. The most curious implement of all was a hefty bat leaning against the wall. We called it the "crap-poker," a necessary tool used to push aside the mounting pile of droppings, thus removing the possibility of accidentally colliding with the previous callers' deposit. Far-fetched or not, this was a way of life. The finishing touch was the writing on the outhouse walls. Every bit of wooden surface within reach of a seated occupant was a display of witticisms, crudely written in pencil. Family secrets adorned these walls, which could have provided some lively material for an aspiring novelist.

When I arrived at the Persson's home, Uncle Pelle introduced me to the outhouse. He took me there on the first night in my new home. We took the long walk, careful not to slip on the snowy path lit by a shining moon. The air was frigid and so was the seat in the outhouse. My bulky winter clothing made it even more difficult to mount the frosty seat. The sparse light seeping through the slats in the door provided the only lighting. After relieving myself I found the cold catalog pages difficult to use; not an easy task for a six-year-old. With steam rising from the depths, I hurriedly pulled my bulky clothing back on and stepped out into the moonlight. Suddenly I felt very homesick, longing for my warm bathroom back home. Uncle Pelle, having used the right-hand side, waited for my re-appearance. Without saying a word, we walked back to the house, hand in hand.

After learning to read Swedish, I was able to decipher some of the outhouse writings, though there were words I couldn't understand. When I asked my teacher what they meant, she raised her eyebrows quizzically, inquiring where I had seen them. I couldn't possibly tell her of their origin, and luckily, she didn't pursue it any further. Not getting an answer from my teacher, I asked a friend to help me out. After telling me their meaning, he, the son of a teacher, told me not to use them publicly. One day I asked Uncle Pelle for a pencil, and he gave me a short stubby one. After seeing me run for the outhouse, he curiously asked me how I might have used the pencil, and I told him that I had written something on the wall. Hearing my story, he broke out laughing, but I could tell by the look on his face that he wasn't pleased.

One day, my side of the outhouse was occupied. For the first time I used the men's toilet and almost fell through the huge hole. With my elbows spread out I managed to catch the seat on either side. What's even more frightening, my bottom landed on the deposits of the previous patron. I was sickened and felt terrible. Ugh! That was my first and last visit to the men's side.

The winter months were even more challenging. We kept a box filled with sand used for spreading a light coating on the slippery path. It saved one from falling on their hind end, particularly during a quick rush to the outhouse which could have been catastrophic. On one starry cold night I had to make a run for it. Hurriedly I pried my bottoms to my ankles and mounted the cold seat, desperately seeking relief. Suddenly I cried out in pain – I had been violated by a frozen turd. The overloaded bucket was at fault. It was time for the crap-poker. Swinging it like a golf club, I managed to break that frozen turd and send it crashing against the wall. From that day on I made sure to never again be impaled by such a nasty object.

Starting School

George is on the far right.

The time had come to start the first grade of the local elementary school. Aunt Sigrid brought me to the single-story schoolhouse, which had two classrooms and a cloakroom in the middle. It was springtime in Ryningsnäs, and the weather was still rather cool. Each classroom was equipped with a potbelly stove providing sufficient heat for comfort. I was introduced to the first and second grade teacher, a single woman named Hilda Ekstrom. She had apparently injured her left eye at one time as it was smaller than the other eye and never quite looked directly at you but wandered back and forth. She was approaching middle age, and her hair was graying. Ms. Ekstrom was a kind woman with a soft voice, and she wore a little hint of a smile as she spoke. She began in the morning with religion, followed by singing, writing, arithmetic, and reading. She was moderately stern and had full control of her class of fifteen students. The children respected her for her strictness and honesty.

The little classroom had three rows of child-sized desks set in rows of five. Each desk had a fold-up top for book storage, an inkwell, and a trough for pencils. Our lunches were left in the cloakroom. The other classroom was for grades three through six, who were taught by Mr. Bernhard Morstam. My classroom had a raised floor in the front of the room for the teacher's desk. An organ was situated on the left side by the window, which was always open during warm weather. World maps hung from the ceiling, placed on rolls which worked much like window shades. The blackboard extended from one wall to the other, with faint guidelines for writing text. It seemed to be quite a cheerful room.

Our class of first graders consisted of five boys and six girls, each assigned our own desk for the duration of the semester. The students came from neighboring farms, and I was so excited to meet my new friends. At first, I seemed to be a curiosity because I was unable to converse very fluently, but I was soon accepted into the group.

Ms. Ekstrom placed me at the front desk in the middle row. She wanted me to be near her, I assume so I could learn Swedish more thoroughly. I couldn't wait to get started with my new school experience. The day started with our teacher playing a hymn on the organ. The hymn, called *"Tryggare kan ingen vara"* (Children of the Heavenly Father), was sung each morning until we all learned it by heart. All the children surrounded the organ while singing this noted hymn. Religious instruction followed and Ms. Ekstrom always had beautiful picture books depicting biblical stories of the life and times of Jesus. She taught us the alphabet, the upper and lower cases in script, and had us write on the blackboard and do assigned classwork during study time. As time went by, I soon learned how to read and was provided with books for reading at home. Ms. Ekstrom was equally gifted in teaching arithmetic, and she made learning fun.

Geography was made easier with the use of the wall maps which depicted faraway countries and the names of principal cities. Blue colors indicated the oceans and green all the lowlands. Various shades of brown revealed the mountains of the world. We were encouraged to draw pictures of birds, flowers, and butterflies. Ms. Ekstrom awarded us stars for good work, and occasionally she would ask for volunteers to read aloud to the class while standing near her desk at the front of the room. The selected readings were nearly always adventure stories. She never needed to raise her voice or scold anyone for misbehaving. Our grades were recorded in a little green book with constructive comments from the teacher. Our parents were required to sign the book indicating that they had reviewed their child's progress.

We played outside during classroom recess. The schoolyard was small and hidden from the highway in a little clearing. A tall flagpole, with the blue and yellow Swedish flag flapping in the wind, stood in the middle of the yard. Also on the school grounds were the teachers' lodgings – Ms. Ekstrom's quarters were upstairs and Mr. Morstam, who was married with six children, lived on the main floor. Every now and then Ms. Ekstrom paid a visit to the creamery, and she was complimentary when she described my progress in her class, which delighted my foster parents. Ms. Ekstrom had accepted an offer to care for a Finnish girl named Britta who arrived in Ryningsnäs in 1942. Britta was a beautiful girl with long blonde hair and sky-blue eyes. She was the apple of all boys' eyes, including mine. I looked forward to these visits as they were a chance to speak Finnish with her and play games while our parents visited over a cup of coffee. I grew very fond of her. She had come from a Swedish-speaking Finnish family in Haaga, a newer district in Helsinki, so speaking Swedish was therefore not a problem for her. But I soon found out that Britta liked the teacher's son, Per, better than me. This was my first childhood crush and I felt aching pangs of jealousy.

Britta thought I was lucky to live with the Perssons in the village. Her life was more sedate, living with a teacher, but she was glad to be there. We spent hours playing in the spacious hallway with the large skylight, and I liked showing her around the farm. We toured the creamery on a Sunday, when it was closed. The storage room, filled with blocks of cheese, seemed to capture her interest, not to mention the chilling room with containers filled with rich cream and yogurt. We played on the sawdust hill above the ice blocks, and we visited the pigsty where she was astonished to see the large sows lying on their sides feeding long rows of piglets. The scurrying rats scared the daylights out of her, and she gave out a little scream and grabbed me around the neck for protection. It was wonderful to be able to comfort her and it filled me with a secret happiness. However, she wanted out of there quickly, not liking the sour-smelling air or the dimly lit corridors, so we walked out hand in hand into the fresh air. I showed her the horse and cow barn, and I could tell that she delighted in the animals. We spent the rest of the afternoon munching on little meatball sandwiches, fresh dairy cheese and butter, delicious cream puffs and coffee. Oh, the benefits of living in a creamery!

Life Around the Creamery

George and Aunt Sigrid.

Aunt Sigrid and Uncle Pelle started their workday early in the morning. It was hard work – lifting heavy milk cans, lugging blocks of fresh cheese to the aging vault, and hauling large blocks of ice from outside to deposit into the cooling tanks. Each piece of equipment that processed milk had to be totally disassembled, scraped, washed, rinsed, and reassembled for the following day, including the pasteurizer, cream separator, the cheese vat and butter churn, all the holding tanks, and the interconnected plumbing. The tile floors also had to be cleaned, and the water hoses were heavy and cumbersome. In addition to the physical labor, Uncle Pelle did the bookkeeping and Aunt Sigrid was the cashier.

By three o'clock in the afternoon they were simply exhausted from their strenuous jobs. Aunt Sigrid would prepare a simple dinner which we ate together most of the time. During their afternoon nap I spent my time playing or wandering around the barns. If I wasn't back by dinnertime Aunt Sigrid left my meal sitting on the kitchen table covered with a towel. Occasionally, I missed eating dinner with my foster folks, but I had no problem eating by myself, though the food was usually cold by the time I got home.

We had a lot of flies in the house since it was so close to the pigsties. Tacky flypaper rolls hung from the ceiling attracted the flies, which easily stuck to the gooey surface. Once trapped, they wiggled with all their might but were unable to escape. When the flypaper became black with dead flies, Aunt Sigrid replenished it with a new roll. Despite this, a few flies usually enjoyed my dinner while I shooed them away. The house was quiet in the afternoon except for occasional snores coming from the other room. I took my time eating dinner because it wasn't all that appetizing: the gravy gelled, the potatoes were dry, and the pork cutlets were tough. However, I had no cause to complain because I had more food here than in Finland and I never had to suffer from hunger pangs.

I did my chores before my foster parents got up from their naps. We had no toilet, running water, or kitchen drains. A pail of water used for drinking and cooking perched on the cupboard next to our wood-burning stove. Everyone in the household used a hanging dipper to take sips of water. When the water was gone, I took the pail downstairs to the pump, hung it on the spout, and started pumping the meter-long handle. It took a few non-producing thrusts until the water began to spurt from the spout. I could only fill it part-way because I couldn't carry a full pail.

The wastewater was next. It contained all the kitchen scraps, potato peels, and other unpleasant objects floating on the surface. The brackish, dark brown water was dumped outside the house into a cesspool behind the pigsty. A perpetual, foul smell wafted from this pond. I tried to be extremely careful when carrying this heavy bucket, but one fateful day I tripped on the steps and watched the contents pour down the staircase and seep into the crevices. It sickened me to see and hear the filthy wastewater splash downstairs. The tumbling bucket made so much noise that it woke Aunt Sigrid from her much-needed sleep. She came running to the staircase and saw the dreadful mess. I was cowering helplessly, waiting for a tongue-lashing which never came. Instead, she was relieved that I hadn't hurt myself and she helped me clean up the mess. It took a lot of work to restore the stairway to its previous condition. This event was a blessing in disguise because it relieved me of this unpleasant chore. After all, that was quite a heavy load for me since I was only a little boy.

Uncle Pelle split the firewood as that was a job for a big man. I carried the chopped wood upstairs and stacked it next to the stove, which burned most of the time, providing us with hot water and a heated surface for cooking. In the wintertime it was used to heat our home. The top surface had a series of rings which could be removed to fit oversized pots. Occasionally the fire burned out completely which meant mornings without breakfast.

As the days passed, Uncle Pelle showed me how the cheese was made. He didn't make it very often, but when the time came to do so he produced many blocks at one time. It was a fascinating process. He filled a huge vat with a soupy mixture of milk and curds. After heating the liquid to the desired temperature, it was drained through a small valve, leaving a crumbly mixture like cottage cheese at the bottom of the vat. Uncle Pelle then used a large scoop to fill several wooden forms, which were lined with cheesecloth, until they were overflowing. The cheesecloth was wrapped over the curds and the forms were then plugged with thick wooden covers. He placed the filled forms into a large press and, by turning a great wheel, he applied pressure to the cover to squeeze out the remainder of the liquid. The forms were then carted to a storage room for drying. After several days the forms were brought out from the storage room and Uncle Pelle removed the cheese cloth to expose a large block of raw cheese. He trimmed the edges neatly and dipped each cheese block into a vat containing hot melted paraffin. After the paraffin set, each block was stamped with a bright red name plate to identify the type of cheese and the day it was manufactured, then they were brought back to the storeroom where the temperature and humidity were carefully controlled. They were too heavy for me to lift, so I watched Uncle Pelle as he handled them with ease. Resembling a library, shelf after shelf lined the storeroom until there were hundreds of cheese blocks on each shelf. Customers had a variety of delectable cheeses from which to choose. Uncle Pelle had gained a good reputation for his cheeses throughout the entire county. I was proud of him and happy that he was my foster dad.

As Sundays were a day of rest and relaxation for Uncle Pelle and Aunt Sigrid, I accompanied them on long afternoon walks. Our walks were limited to dry summer days since the road became muddy and full of ruts when it rained. We always dressed in our Sunday best, Uncle Pelle in black slacks and a white jacket with his official-looking visor cap, and Aunt Sigrid in her flower print dress and nylons with white-heeled shoes. Aunt Sigrid was fairly quiet, though her wonderful sense of humor kept us entertained and she always laughed at our antics. I wore my short black pants, a long-sleeved black jacket, and a visor cap. We enjoyed walking along the country roads, sometimes picking wildflowers or whittling green tree branches into little whistles. Uncle Pelle showed me how to whittle branches of different lengths – the longer the whistle the lower the pitch.

George with neighbor women.

George dancing with neighbor girls.

A New Nest

During the summer I played outside as much as I could. Since our home was so small it didn't afford much space for my personal items or toys. Aunt Sigrid had moved my bedroom to the kitchen which gave us all more privacy, and I was no longer awakened by their early rising. The wooden sofa became my new bed. To open it I had to lift off the wooden top and lean it against the wall, then slide the bottom out to expose a straw-filled mattress. It was more comfortable than my previous bed. During the night I was frequently woken up by the sound of mice scurrying within the walls. I eventually got used to these nocturnal critters.

Though mousetraps were placed throughout the house, there were always more mice than traps so catching them was an ongoing battle.

A line of storage sheds was located about a hundred yards from our house, filled with discarded household items and used machinery from the creamery. One shed was nearly empty and contained only old burlap sacks, clothing, and junk. I asked Uncle Pelle if I could play there. He walked out with me one day to have a look around and said that if I could somehow clean it out then I could claim it as my own. I spent many days cleaning up the place and even burned some of the refuse, causing a terrible stench. In addition, the smell of the nearby slaughterhouse sometimes lingered for days, making it a little unpleasant. However, once the shed was clear I borrowed a bucket and a scrub brush from the creamery and busied myself swabbing the floor. The walls were equally dirty, covered with spider webs and nails. Little by little I cleaned up the shed to my satisfaction. Aunt Sigrid found some scatter rugs to cover the plank floor, and she let me choose from her collection of bric-a-brac. I put wooden crates to good use as tables for storing my books and other treasures. I filled small glass jars with wildflowers and even found an old mirror and attached it to the wall.

After weeks of working, Aunt Sigrid paid me a visit during a break from the creamery. She was pleasantly surprised to see my little home away from home and she began bringing me goodies including glasses of yogurt and samples of cheese. She also brought Uncle Pelle for a visit, and he was absolutely astonished with my work. Occasionally, I would spend the night out there, sleeping on an old cot scrounged from one of the neighbors. I also borrowed candles to make it more cozy after dark when I had time to read books lent to me by Ms. Ekstrom. It didn't take long before I had a captive audience of neighbor kids visiting me at all hours.

One special memory is of Sweden's Midsummer Festival which is celebrated outdoors with singing and dancing around the customary Maypole. Usually, a large tree is felled, and all the branches trimmed off, then it is decorated with flowers and ferns. A cross bar is fitted near the top of the pole from which hang two circular wreathes made of flowers and branches. With the help of several strong men, the pole is erected and placed in a deep hole in the ground. The village folk attended this annual festival, drinking and dancing round and round to the music of violins and accordions playing polkas and schottisches. The kids eagerly joined in and danced their hearts out. Not to be left out, I constructed my own Maypole with the help of the neighbor girls. It was set outside my shed, and though much smaller than the main pole, it was just as fun. Aunt Sigrid brought us a large pitcher of fruit juice and joined our festivities. We had so much fun singing and dancing around our miniature Maypole.

Not having a radio, much less a television set, was no setback. When left to our own devices and imaginations, we kids never had time to be bored. Lessons learned in childhood served me well later in life.

The Agronomer

The agronomer was a colossal man, a towering figure with an authoritarian voice. He was always impeccably dressed in light brown, tweed knickerbocker suits with a matching visor cap. He moved impressively, swinging a walking cane, and his voice, which was low and gravelly, commanded respect. When speaking to an individual he would look directly into their eyes, as if probing into their inner self. His hands were clean and soft and the fingernails, never having seen a day's labor, were perfectly manicured. His hair, graying at the temples, was always neatly combed, and his pale pink face showed slight creases as if burdened by heavy thoughts. He was feared and revered by all the village workers.

The agronomer's personal property occupied some ten acres, and his home, an impressive three-story structure, sat on a hilltop shrouded by stately oak trees. From a distance his home resembled a small castle with round black turrets. The grounds were impeccably landscaped with sculpted bushes and beautiful flower beds. The gravel walkway leading to his home was perfectly graded, and an impressive fruit grove occupied the south side of the property. Neat rows of apple, pear, and cherry trees lined the sloping hillside, well-suited to the southern climate of Småland.

The agronomer had a complete household staff. His chief cook, an amiable middle-aged woman, kept her staff busy from early morning till evening catering to his circle of important friends and business partners. The kitchen was spacious with two wood-burning stoves capable of handling eight pots at a time. His servants kept his home in fastidious shape; no one, with the exception of his staff, had ever set foot into every room, numbering in the dozens. He owned two large black dogs which were trained to keep the grounds safe from curious intruders. He knew of no discomforts as his needs were always fulfilled.

The village workers made weekly visits to the big house to collect their wages. Everyone stood in line to greet the landowner at his expansive desk, exchanged a few words with him, and then collected their pay. He counted each worker's wages very carefully, handing out the cash and following with a hardy handshake. His low voice filled the grand room with its exquisite furnishings. This room was the only one the villagers ever saw, and upon receiving their pay they filed out quickly and quietly.

The agronomer was known to show up at various work sites unannounced and he never criticized his workers. His laborers worked hard in all their endeavors, be it field work, caring for livestock, running the creamery, or manning the blacksmith shop. Since he was a fair man with a commanding presence, the villagers looked up to him for his leadership.

My first encounter with him occurred outside our creamery one sunny day when he paid an unannounced visit to the Persson family. I had just turned seven that February of 1942 and was playing at the dairy entrance where the farmers would bring their milk wagons to the loading platform. I was trying to climb an old oak tree by the drive when I heard a deep voice below me. I turned quickly and jumped down from the tree. Dressed in his customary garb, he addressed me with that deep voice and extended his large hand, inviting me to shake it. As I met his hand, he suddenly flipped it behind my small one. I tried shaking his hand again and found him flipping his hand behind mine, time after time. At last, he grabbed my hand and shook it gently. As he grinned at me, looking down, towering over me, he asked about my plans for the summer. Before I could answer he looked me sternly and directly in the eyes and said, "Matti, I will hire you to work on my farm this summer starting next Monday. The vegetable fields need a lot of caretaking and I have just the job for you. Here, in my village, little boys don't have time to play around and flitter away the summer with childishness. There's work to be done and I need your help. We here in Sweden are taking good care of many Finnish children, you included. We are feeding you, protecting you from the ravages of war in your home country, and teaching you in our schools. In return, I'm expecting you to work very hard for me and I will pay you accordingly." Of course, I was frightened of this immense man and his commanding voice. His shoes were extremely large and being a small boy and thus close to the ground, I was even more scared.

There was no way of saying no. I stuttered and stammered but accepted the job offer unconditionally. He then strolled off swinging his luxurious walking cane, while I stood there totally stunned by his visit and excited about the prospect of working side by side with the other villagers.

Early Monday morning I found myself at the vegetable field. Row upon long row of freshly planted carrots stretched into the distance. They needed thinning so the taller plants could mature into succulent veggies. I was shown how to go about the process of thinning and weeding. I soon learned how to use the trowel, loosening the dirt and removing handfuls of little carrot starts, leaving the larger carrot plants intact. I straddled the first row on my knees and went to work. It was slow and awkward at first but soon became natural. My fellow worker, an experienced farmer, gave me much needed encouragement and thus we worked side by side for many hours. I was dressed in short knee pants and a short sleeve shirt, and my feet had become tough as leather from walking around barefoot. Looking ahead, the rows of carrots converged together in the distance. I worked as hard as I possibly could, but every time I looked up it seemed that I had hardly made any headway. I quickly fell behind my friend and was not able to keep up. The sun's rays warmed my back and I soon felt rivers of sweat pouring down my torso. My back hurt, as did my knees, and the day dragged on. Finally, it was high noon and lunchtime. Aunt Sigrid had fixed a couple of fried egg sandwiches and a bottle of milk. Oh boy, that really hit the spot. I finished my lunch by munching on a red apple. Then it was back to work.

The evening rolled around, and it was time to go home. I had thinned three rows of carrots and found myself at the far end of the field, making my return trip that much longer. My back ached, I was dead-tired, and I hated the agronomer. I was even too tired to eat dinner. My straw bed never felt as good as it did after that first day's work. We were paid a flat rate by the row, so since my thinning rate was rather dismal compared to my experienced friend, there was much room for improvement.

I worked the fields for three summer months, six days a week, thinning and picking ripened carrots and potatoes. A horse-drawn plow, resembling a rotating propeller with curved blades, dug up the potatoes, scattering them over the field. Another horse-drawn flatbed wagon followed, loaded with empty wicker baskets large enough to hold some fifty pounds of potatoes each. We picked them from morning 'till dusk filling basket after basket. They were then loaded and brought to a large, underground root cellar for storage. At the end of the first week, Uncle Pelle and I walked up to the agronomer's house to collect our pay, and I gleefully received my very first cash payment for my work. It was a wonderful feeling, getting all this money for my hard labor. I gave my money to Uncle Pelle for safekeeping, and I found out much later that he had put it aside to buy a new suit and shoes for my return trip to Finland.

In the countryside.

A New Season

My first summer in Sweden passed and the cool fall weather came creeping in. It was time again for us children to don our shoes and socks. The first few days were sheer murder, as our feet had grown and become tough from walking barefoot the entire summer. It was difficult to walk because the shoes were stiff and uncomfortable. It took time to readjust to them. The days became shorter and much colder, making it uncomfortable to walk to school in the blustery weather. On rainy days the cloakroom smelled of water-soaked jackets, much like a wet dog.

I had mastered the Swedish language at last. My second school year found me sitting in a different row assigned to second graders. Ms. Ekstrom taught each class alternately. After putting the first graders to work writing lessons she would turn her attention to the second graders and teach them a different lesson, maybe arithmetic or social studies. Being in school was a lot of fun. Reading came easily to me and what's more, I loved it. Ms. Ekstrom allowed me to borrow some of her books about the Stone Age and early caveman dwellings which had pictures of petroglyphs carved on the walls. Many of her books were well-illustrated which caused my interest in reading to climb to new heights. My life in Sweden was off to a good start. I rarely thought about Finland, nor did I hear about the raging war on the European mainland, or about the killing of innocent people and the destruction of homes and factories. Much of this can be attributed to the lack of radios and newspapers. Sweden, a neutral country, was a haven, unlike the rest of Europe.

In my third year at school, I left Ms. Ekstrom's class and moved across the hall to Mr. Morstam's classroom. His room was larger with four rows of seats, the first row for the third grade and so on. I found my new seat near the door. The pressure was building as the older students treated the new ones like scrubs, with the expected jeers and rude comments. Mr. Morstam quickly put an end to that. He was a soft-spoken man, a man of authority who commanded respect. He was tall, slim, and always well-dressed in a suit and tie. He wore a hearing aid with a long, thin line leading to a pocketed battery which was barely noticeable.

Mr. Morstam taught all four classes at one time. He started each day with a general lecture and proceeded to assign work to each grade level. He would then concentrate on different subjects, covering all grade work accordingly. It must have been time-consuming to prepare each day's lessons and then to correct the homework papers, but he had mastered this method of teaching over the years. Mr. Morstam's class did not have an organ, but we could hear Ms. Ekstrom playing hers every morning during the religious hour. Our first class of the day was also religious instruction during which students chosen by the teacher read selected Bible verses. Some Bible verses were committed to memory. Since Ryningsnäs lacked a church, the responsibility to provide religious education to children fell upon the school.

Speaking of church, my foster parents were not regular churchgoers but would sometimes bicycle to church in Mörlunda, a neighboring town. I sat on the back of Uncle Pelle's bike, and when stopping to rest or to walk up a hill, I could feel how my poor buttocks would become completely numb from the long ride. Hopping off the bike to walk, I could not feel the earth beneath my feet and sometimes stumbled and fell to the ground. One day we rode the bikes there to attend the funeral of a long-time friend of Uncle Pelle. The white church with its tall steeple, fitted with tolling bells, also had a graveyard with markers of names and dates going back some hundred years. The minister, an old white-haired man, preached from a high pulpit attached to the wall of the church. His funeral sermon made me fall soundly asleep and Aunt Sigrid had to poke me repeatedly to keep me awake. Following services, the minister greeted us at the door to shake hands. He had the softest hands in the world, and they were snowy white. He certainly lacked the hands of the common farmer. I always looked forward to shaking his hand – I swear they were softer than velvet. The trip home seemed easier, for much of the road was downhill. The passing cars stirred up the road dust and we were pretty grubby by the trip's end. I'm rather glad that our church trips were few and far between.

At school, Mr. Morstam lent me books to read at home. Most of them were nonfiction, about life on the farm. He even had books about the stars and the solar system. Mrs.

Morstam often invited me to stay for dinner with their family. Gunnar, their oldest son, was a sixth grader and would soon be graduating and moving on to an intermediate school away from Ryningsnäs. He hoped to become a teacher, like his father. Mr. Morstam never showed favoritism toward his eldest son but treated him the same as the rest of the children. Per, their youngest son, became my best friend. We played together after school and Per taught me many games he learned from his older brothers and sisters.

Even though Ryningsnäs was a small country town, four children from Finland came to live there during the war years. Rolf had lived on the outskirts of Helsinki and as his parents were well-to-do, it didn't come as much of a surprise when he ended up living in a large, country home in Sweden. It could have been a simple coincidence, but he was indeed fortunate. The grounds of his residence were adorned with manicured shrubs and the formal driveway framed with beautiful trees. The three-story house had rooms to spare, with maids and porters taking care of every detail. However, Rolf would be put to work with his own list of chores. He was a hard worker and fit in perfectly with his foster parents and servants.

Goran and another boy from the farmlands of Finland ended up living with a rural family. They harvested hay and sold it to neighboring farms as feed for livestock. Their home was modest with several outbuildings designed for storing cut hay, workhorses, and farming implements. During the summer Goran learned to work the fields, cutting hay with a horse-drawn cutter. He was a rough and tough boy. We got along and spoke Finnish to each other, but as time passed, the Finnish was forgotten, and Swedish became our official language. I didn't see these boys very often outside of school since their homes were far from the agronomer's spread.

One cold winter day during our lunch break, Goran, Rolf, and I went exploring down by the shallow lake near the schoolhouse. The weather had cooled to freezing over the last couple of weeks, and the snow-covered schoolgrounds glistened in the sparkling sun. The lake was frozen solid and the tall grass tips poked through the ice near the shoreline. The air was brisk, and it just made one feel alive. We were attracted by the slick, icy surface and tested the strength of it by throwing rocks, trying to break it. The ice held firm and the rocks slid harmlessly away. Goran, the biggest of us, found a long wooden post and tried to crack the surface. Nothing. The water seemed frozen solid, so one by one we stepped out onto the lake. It held. Gaining courage, we made our way further from the shore. Our excitement reached fever pitch. It was laborious to walk on the smooth surface with our leather-bottomed shoes, like three little penguins wobbling around. Oh boy, this was fun! We had waddled out some distance when we suddenly heard a creaking sound beneath our feet. Cautiously, we fanned out, trying to ease the weight, but the ice began to yield under each step. It was like a magical carpet. Moving on the ice caused it to buckle but it held long enough, enabling us to take another step. The strange manner of the rubbery ice should have been a sign of danger, but the novelty of it pushed us on. The recess bell was ringing to summon the students back to class, but a few curious stragglers remained watching as we clowned about on the frozen lake. One of them ran into the schoolhouse to tattle to Mr. Morstam.

As I turned toward the shore, the ice began to crumble with each step. Water seeped onto the surface and made walking even more difficult. The ice buckled and swayed, but by moving faster I managed to keep ahead of the breaking surface. Having been summoned from the classroom, Mr. Morstam quickly appeared by the shore. He fearlessly stepped out onto the ice and reached for my hand, pulling me out of danger. Goran and Rolf were not so lucky, being further out on the threatening ice. Rolf, seeing the trouble that I had experienced, headed for the shore along a different path and made it back without incident. But Goran, being the farthest out, wasn't as lucky. The crumbling ice finally broke under his heavy weight, causing him to crash through. And down he went into the icy water. We heard him screaming for help as he clutched the edge of the ice. Luckily, his feet reached the bottom of the shallow lake, but he was unable to pull himself from the watery trap. Mr. Morstam ran back to the schoolhouse to get a long rope and rushed back as quickly as possible, hurling the coiled rope in Goran's direction. On the third try Goran caught it and held on with all his might, but he was unable to pull himself from the icy hole. Finally, Rolf and I helped Mr. Morstam pull Goran from the water. Weakened from the cold, Goran lay on top of the buckling ice as we pulled him across the surface like a bagged sea lion. He was shivering and in a state of shock as we managed to half carry, half drag him to the schoolhouse. Quickly he was undressed in front of the potbelly stove and covered with a warm blanket. Curious kids surrounded him and stared at the hapless and somewhat embarrassed Goran, sitting by the hot stove, his body still shivering as he tried to warm up.

The normally calm Mr. Morstam gave the three of us the lecture of our lives. Our respective foster parents would be notified, but luckily our grades would not be affected. "Those Finns, what crazy kids they are!" they would say amongst themselves. Needless to say, we had learned our lesson, though Goran became a hero of sorts, and his story of the wintry incident became more and more embellished with each telling.

The Nightingale

Every now and then something wonderful happened in our village. These were the totally unplanned events which brought us surprising moments in our busy rural lives. One such event was the appearance of the nightingale, a tiny bird which inhabits the forest undergrowth. The nightingale is well-camouflaged with its russet-colored upper parts and whitish underside. Its eyes are large and black, and its beak resembles that of a pincer, useful for catching insects. One seldom, if ever, hears its melodious song in the daytime; its concerts are scheduled for late evening following dusk. Once it finds a suitable place to roost it tends to return to the same spot year after year, though the exact location of its nest is usually a mystery. For this reason, the villagers were forever ready to seek out this mystical bird.

One day, Elsa, the wife of the village blacksmith, excitedly announced that she thought she had heard the nightingale while she was riding home on her bicycle one evening. She heard something in the woods and when she stopped and listened quietly, she was suddenly rewarded with a beautiful trill, so melodious and distinct that it took her breath away. Early the following morning she excitedly related her experience to her neighbors and since she was considered a trustworthy source of news, some of us decided to pay the bird a visit. We organized a small group and after supper we strolled through the warm, calm night to the spot Elsa had described. She led the way, cautioning us to be very quiet.

We could hear the crickets everywhere and an occasional hoot from an owl. The gravel road crunched beneath the adults' shoes, and Elsa kept quieting us down as we approached the spot where she had heard the singing bird. The stars illuminated the night and any traffic on the infrequently traveled road had subsided. There we stood, holding our breath. Not a sound could be heard. We waited and waited, casting suspicious glances at Elsa. As soon as several villagers turned back for home, considering the evening a lost cause, the first burst of the nightingale's trill came forth, followed by a long interval of total silence. Then, we heard that incredible bird as she sang her heart out, altering the trills, singing with such clarity and detail. The concert went on for many delicious moments. My skin was covered with goosebumps, and I could feel shivers coursing up and down my spine. Sometimes in life these minute happenings bring so much satisfaction and enjoyment. One tends to lose these infinitesimal opportunities, even though we are surrounded by them; we simply need to take the time to recognize them. This experience with a tiny, magical bird had a profound impact on my outlook on life.

Village Friends

George with friends, Goran and Rolf.

Tutte, another friend in the village, lived with his mom and dad and his older brother Roland in a small house down the road from our dairy. His father was often drunk, his mother seemed brow-beaten, and Roland was somewhat of a bully. But the blonde-haired, brown-eyed Tutte was always friendly with me. Tutte's father worked the hay wagons, bringing the dried hay to the lofts above the animal barns. Large, vacuum-operated ducts sucked the hay from the wagons and blew it into the loft until it reached the ceiling. The ample hay supply was saved for the winter months providing food for the horses and dairy cows. The hay could simply be dropped into the barn below from strategically placed trap doors.

Tutte and I played in the hayloft, jumping over and over from the roof rafters into the softly packed hay. Particles of hay stuck to our sweaty bodies making us itch horribly and leaving us with an uncomfortable rash which lasted for several days. But that was a small price to pay for the fun we had. We once found a pitchfork half hidden in the hay which could have been dangerous, if not fatal, had we landed on top of it, but being kids, it didn't stop us from having fun.

Tutte's dad also took care of all the outhouses, exchanging full "honey buckets" for empty ones. Most of the outhouses had trap doors behind the structure for this purpose. The full containers, each weighing over seventy pounds, were cumbersome to lift onto the horse-drawn flatbed cart, so it took two men to perform this task. They were hauled to a local dump some distance from the village. Usually, these jobs were done by laborers not suited for more demanding tasks. Tutte's dad was, at times, ridiculed behind his back; he didn't seem to be well-liked, and he made no effort to be nice to his neighbors. However, my foster parents taught me to respect my elders regardless of their station in life, and that included Tutte's dad. Tutte and I got along fine – he was more a follower than an innovator. He didn't go to school and therefore could not read or write, and he seemed engrossed with his daydreams much of the time. His family life was surely a factor. When his dad got drunk, Tutte shied away from his home.

I remained friends with Tutte during my stay in Sweden. He stayed close to home, and I was curious why he didn't attend school. Tutte's brother Roland kept getting into all kinds of trouble and no one seemed to like him much. He seemed to enjoy being a troublemaker, and once he was even caught stealing chickens. I was afraid of him and tried to steer clear as much as possible, even though Tutte reassured me that he was harmless. At times Roland had a mean streak which caused him to drive his younger brother to tears. That entire family was suspected of skullduggery. Ryningsnäs had no law enforcement officers, not even a sheriff's deputy. Rather, folks looked after each other and maintained the peace in the village.

A Colorful Visit

One day the wandering gypsies[5] came to Ryningsnäs with their horse-drawn carts and pitched their tents along the side of the main road, not far from the railroad station. The women were dressed in full black skirts, white fluffy blouses, and colorful bandanas. The men wore brown pants and white shirts with black hats adorning their heads at jaunty angles. They came to entertain the local folks and played strange-sounding musical instruments. They were excellent dancers, twirling merrily to the music. Their children wandered around the visiting crowds looking for handouts and small change. Tutte and I went to see the gypsies one evening. Having heard that they were notorious pickpockets[6] we were mindful of keeping our hands in our pockets to protect what little money we had. The villagers believed that a gypsy could never be trusted, even though they brought a lot of excitement to our otherwise simple lives. Festivities began in the evening when pungent-smelling

[5] Now referred to as Roma or Romani, as the term 'gypsy' is considered a pejorative by some.
[6] A negative stereotype common to the historical time of this story.

carbide lamps lit up their campground. A large, black pot, boiling over an open fire and filled with (no doubt) a witch's brew, emitted an inviting aroma which wafted throughout the campsite. Tutte and I took a chance to taste it and found it surprisingly good. The ingredients were unknown, though some local dogs had gone missing and may have ended up in that pot. A fortune teller drew curious spectators who were willing to part with a few coins to learn about their luck with love and riches. The gypsies remained on their campsite for several days, and when the visitors stopped coming, they packed up their wagons and headed out of town in search of new opportunities.

Sex Education

The village barn held more than forty horses and two hundred dairy cows. The workhorses were used to pull heavy hay wagons and farming equipment. They worked hard and were invaluable to the agronomer. His two stallions, a draft horse and the other a beautiful riding horse, kept the population intact. Neighboring farmers often brought their mares here to be impregnated. The agronomer also had riding horses which he used for his personal pleasure. Sometimes he invited friends on fox hunts and volunteered these magnificent steeds to his eager hunter friends. But most of the time he rode his personal horse to oversee his workers who toiled in the surrounding fields.

The dairy cows provided enough milk to keep Ryningsnäs supplied with various dairy products. The feeding of all these animals was no small job. Our barns were equipped with moving trolleys coursing down the middle aisle between the two rows of livestock. The feed troughs were filled by barn laborers pitching hay, alfalfa, and a cardboard-like substance high in fiber.

The dairy barn used modern milking machines and great care was taken when attaching the milkers to the cows.

The teats were washed and hosed off carefully before being attached to the milking machine. The milk was poured into large, stainless-steel cans and transported to the creamery by a horse drawn cart. When not helping Uncle Pelle in the creamery I went to the barn to watch the action. It was a lot of fun to see the cows being milked. Sven was one of the workers tending to the livestock and he showed me how to attach the milkers on the cows' teats and how to milk a cow by hand. With practice, I could soon squirt the milk directly into the face of the barn cat. Some cows were quite uncooperative and would swing their dirty tails all about. Being hit in the face with a cow's tail was pretty disgusting.

The newborn calves had their own section in the barn. Seeing the emerging wet head of the newborn calf appear kept me wide-eyed with wonder. The little calf was licked clean by the seemingly proud mother. The vet, an old friend of the agronomer, usually came to assist. The calf was so cute, and it didn't take very long before it was able to stand on its own shaky feet. Sven told me to put my hand into its mouth, and it latched onto my fingers and sucked them with enthusiastic pulls. Its tongue was rough like sandpaper.

Living on a farm can be quite educational for children and it's a wonderful way to learn about the birds and the bees. Our parents never talked about such things and Aunt Sigrid and Uncle Pelle were no exception. Children learned about sex by observing the goings on at the farm. Now and then a neighboring farmer came to visit, bringing his mare to be "serviced" by our accomplished stallion, creating curiosity among the farm hands as well as us kids. On one such day my friends and I happened to be around to witness a mating ritual between a mare and our stallion. Not knowing what to expect, we gathered around the horse barn to observe.

Sven brought the stallion out from the barn. He was beautiful, arrogant, and well-groomed, with his hide shining in the sunlight. He pranced proudly as he was led to meet his mate. He made deep grunting noises as they met nose to nose. The mare had been carefully prepared, her ankles tied with leather straps extending around her neck, preventing her from kicking and injuring the stallion, and her tail was tethered. When Sven saw us kids standing there he cussed loudly, telling us to go away, that this was no place for us. We walked off reluctantly, but we didn't go far. We were going to watch this exhibition one way or another. Curiosity has a way of solving things. Had Sven looked in our direction he would have seen four curious little heads poking out from behind the corner of the barn.

Sven continued prepping the stallion. After exchanging a few hurried words with the visiting farmer, he led him behind the mare to allow him to pick up her strong scent. Suddenly, to our surprise, the stud's penis dropped from hiding and began to grow, inch by inch, longer and longer. The stallion reared on his strong back legs and mounted the mare. Wide-eyed and holding our breath, we watched this incredible performance. The stallion bucked and pushed, with its front feet encircling the female. After some time, he emitted an unnatural-sounding cry, then shook his enormous head and slowly dismounted. No longer erect, his penis began to shrink and disappear from our sight. We were totally spellbound and didn't really understand what we had just witnessed.

A couple of days later I hinted to Sven what I had seen and begged him to tell me more about it. He was a little upset by my confession but admitted to me that it was time I learned about farm life. He told me that the mare might become pregnant and give birth to a foal. I didn't believe him at first but took his word anyway. As time passed, I saw the bulls mating with the cows, the male pig thrusting his corkscrew-shaped appendage while mating with the female, and well, suddenly it seemed like everyone was doing it.

The Spyglass

When I arrived in Sweden, I brought one little suitcase with me which held my very carefully selected personal possessions. Due to weight and size restrictions I had to leave most of my goodies behind. My prized possession happened to be my spyglass. A magnifying glass was a better description, but "spyglass" sounded much more exciting. All my friends in Finland owned one and it seemed like a standard accessory of every boy, like a slingshot or a pocketknife. Aunt Sylvi had given it to me for my birthday. We used our spyglasses in attempts to burn paper, cloth, or old negatives by focusing the sun's bright rays directly onto the selected items. Most materials, like paper or cloth, only smoldered, emitting little wisps of smoke, but some film negatives burst into flame quite readily, though it was difficult to find the right kind of film. We were forever trying to burn different materials in the hopes of finding the real McCoy. For the most part however, a spyglass was considered a harmless toy.

Tutte and I spent a lot of time together and we sometimes got into trouble with our shenanigans. Before I started working the vegetable fields, I spent my summer playing all day long. I had pretty much forgotten all about my spyglass until one day I found it in my box of goodies while playing out in the shed. I pocketed it and went over to Tutte's house, then we took off for the woods. I was eager to show it to him since he had never seen one before. I took some wood shavings and a few old negatives with me, and I told Tutte how it worked. He got excited as we found a large rock and stuffed the shavings into a little crevice, covering it with the film. Tutte didn't believe me when I told him we were going to start a small fire.

The sun was shining brightly that day as I took my spyglass and focused the sun's rays directly on the film. Tutte watched with interest and when he saw a curly wisp of smoke, he became extra excited. A small hole formed, bubbling at the edges, and without warning, the film ignited.

"Success!" I cried gleefully. The wood shavings erupted into flame, and we both cheered with enthusiasm. We put more shavings on the fire and added twigs and leaves. Then, unexpectedly, a strong gust of wind fueled the fire even more, igniting the dry moss on the outcropping, which caught on fire. Before we knew what was happening, the surrounding dry bushes near the rock ignited with a roar. We were terrified as the fire gained strength, now totally out of control. We could only stare as it grew. The nearest trees exploded into flames. Panic-stricken, we ran away, scared out of our wits. The Johnson's house was not far away from the burning site, and we feared the worst. We ran back to the village to get help.

The black smoke from the burning forest could now be seen from the village. Alarmed farmhands armed with shovels and buckets raced toward the billowing black smoke. I ran to the creamery to fetch Uncle Pelle who was luckily almost done hosing down the floor. I hurriedly told him what had happened. He looked down at me angrily, grabbed a couple of buckets, gave me one to carry, and we raced to the woods toward the burning forest. Luckily, the wind had shifted, forcing the flames away from the Johnsons' house. We started pumping water from the Johnson's well and soon a bucket brigade was formed in attempts to quell the fire. Our efforts seemed hopeless at first, but fortunately the small thin forest was bounded by the village road in one direction and the main rural road in the other. Once the fire had consumed most of the young trees, and with the help of the fire-fighting villagers, it slowed to a smoldering stretch of once-beautiful forest land. To say that we were lucky to have contained the fire would be an understatement. The wind worked in our favor and thanks to the instant response of the villagers we had certainly escaped a major catastrophe. Fortunately, the fire hadn't touched the Johnsons' home.

Uncle Pelle, now extremely angry, confronted me with burning questions regarding the fire. Fearing a major spanking, I told him tearfully how I had wanted to show Tutte how to start a fire using my spyglass. Of course, it was not my intention to burn down an entire forest. I apologized repeatedly, but Uncle Pelle nevertheless confiscated my spyglass and locked it in his desk. Uncle Pelle reported the story to the agronomer and convinced him that he would take the necessary disciplinary actions. After all, he was responsible for me being there.

For months following this near tragic incident, Uncle

Pelle would remind me of my dastardly act whenever we passed the charred remains of the little forest. His comments of "See what you did!" made me cringe inside. My face would turn red with shame, and I found it difficult to swallow. I had learned my lesson well and would remember it for the rest of my life.

First Drink

It was a gorgeous summer day, not a cloud in the sky. We were walking on the main rural road clad only in our swimming trunks. We had been playing and splashing in our favorite swimming hole in the Em River. It was one of the few safe places along the river protected from the swift-moving current, located across the river from the railroad station and the grocery store. We crossed back to the main rural road over a narrow wooden bridge, wide enough for horse-drawn wagons. I had met with Rolf, Goran, and Per for the day, and now homeward bound, we took our time poking along the road. As we trudged along, we saw a man ahead of us lugging a two-gallon jug of mead that he had purchased from the store. Mead, an alcoholic liquor made of fermented honey, yeast and water, and spiked with fruit and malt, was frequently served with meals. It is quite tasty but intoxicating if drunk to excess. The man carried it on one shoulder for a while, soon switching to the other shoulder. His heavy burden tired him out so he put the jug on the ground to rest for a while. Our curiosity aroused, we slowed up, remaining a safe distance behind him. Again, he picked up his load, this time cradling it like a baby, and continued his journey, alternately carrying the jug on one shoulder then the other.

After resting awhile, he suddenly picked up the jug and stepped into the woods, then reappeared shortly after without the jug and continued onward at a brisk pace. Apparently, he decided to go home for his cart and return to this spot to retrieve the jug later. We watched, fascinated, and when the man was out of sight, we stepped into the woods to figure out where he hid the mead. We were on the verge of giving up our hunt when Per found it nestled behind a mossy rock. Gee whiz, what to do? Rolf, the self-appointed leader, suggested that we carry the jug somewhere else to try it, though we all knew what mead tasted like, having sipped it from time to time with dinner. Taking turns, we lugged our prize deeper into the woods to a clearing next to a little creek. We hoisted the huge bottle on top of a stump and pried open the reusable stopper. Rolf was the first to take a swig. He grinned from ear to ear, wiping his face. Then we all joined in taking a long pull. Hey, this was really fun! Repeatedly we passed the bottle, not realizing its intoxicating effects. We ran around like little foals, whinnying and laughing. We stomped in and out of the creek, stripped naked, and ran around with abandon. My cheeks were sore from the continuous laughter. We were having a ball, but I was getting dizzy. In fact, we were all dizzy like storming geese on a rampage. We must have consumed over half of the contents of the jug. Not being able to take another swig, we closed the stopper and hid the jug for another day. We parted bearing silly grins on our faces and staggered to our respective homes.

When I arrived home, Aunt Sigrid and Uncle Pelle were snoring in their room, taking their afternoon nap. My dinner was sitting on the kitchen table, covered as always. I wasn't a bit hungry, but boy was I dizzy. I lay down on the kitchen bench and fell soundly asleep. Aunt Sigrid, finding me lying on that hard surface, opened the bench and stuffed me on the straw bed. My "lights" were totally out. I woke up suddenly in the dark and vomited with a vengeance, all over my bed and myself and on the kitchen floor. Aunt Sigrid, awakened by the noise, came running into the kitchen, now ripe with the smell of vomit. She seemed alarmed over my predicament and quickly tried to clean me up the best she could. Not having a bathroom in the house made it so much more difficult. After changing the bed sheets, she put me back for a restless slumber. I woke up in the morning with a horrendous headache and stomach cramps. I ran outside, past the outdoor pump, the row of sheds and the slaughterhouse to the outhouse where I suffered all alone with diarrhea and a massive headache.

Again, it was time for a confession. Uncle Pelle and Aunt Sigrid must have been thoroughly disappointed with their Finnish kid whom they had so lovingly accepted with open arms. But, bypassing corporal punishment or a severe tongue lashing, they left me alone – a first hangover was a bitter punishment. Oh, how I suffered the entire day. I think that I really wanted to die more than anything else.

With no telephones to transmit news in the village, the milk runs offered a dependable means of communication. Thus, the fate of Rolf and Goran came to light during the morning milk delivery. They had fared worse than I, having messed up their beds with diarrhea. It was impossible to keep any news secret in this simple country village. Their parents opted to tenderize their already sore bottoms with a leather belt. In the end, I was the luckiest of the three of us. We never heard how Per had faired. Mr. Morstam, the schoolteacher, wasn't talking. Once again, having gotten into trouble, I had found yet another bitter pill with which to build character for the future. As for the hapless farmer returning for his jug of mead, I could only imagine the look of bewilderment on his face.

Electric Fence

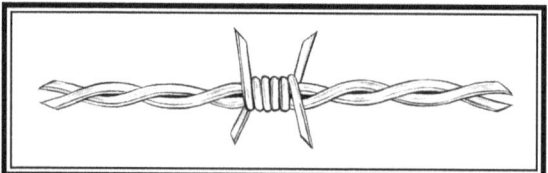

Here we were, living in the 1940s, in a neutral country, more or less oblivious to the horrible war raging on in the rest of Europe. The only hint of war was an occasional shortage of certain commodities. It had become difficult to obtain barbed wire used for fencing in livestock, and as our fencing began to break down due to rust or foraging by the horses or cows, replacement fencing could not be purchased. The village blacksmith, who had less than a sixth-grade education, was an incredibly smart man. What he lacked in book learning he more than made up for with innate intelligence and wisdom. Understanding the situation, he suggested that the barbed wiring be replaced with a single line hooked up to an electrical power source. Once he sold his idea to the agronomer, he was permitted to carry out his plan. The worn-out barbed wire was replaced with a single strand of metal attached to the existing posts with insulated connectors. The blacksmith was able to obtain batteries with which to charge the line. Having completed the installation of the first electric fence in the village, it was time to test its efficacy. The blacksmith made a final hookup to the battery and then turned on the "juice." Nearby villagers gathered to watch this dedication of sorts, and the blacksmith asked for volunteers to join hands, forming a long human chain.

I happened to be standing barefoot near the last man in this human chain, curiously watching the ongoing events. Without a warning, the man suddenly reached out, grabbed my small hand, and held on with a vise-like grip. The electrified fence sprang to life, sending a whopping jolt which raced through the human chain and terminated in my body. Not only was I barefooted, but it had rained earlier in the day leaving the ground wet and filled with small puddles. The electrical conductivity could not have been better. My body made a direct electrical grounding path and, being the terminus to this human chain, the maximum jolt of electricity coursed through my small frame. The stupendous shock came in pulses as our hands jerked in unison. I tried to cry out in pain but was too stunned by the repeated jolts of electricity. As the current traveled up and down my body, it felt as if water rushed through my veins. It was excruciating, the worst pain I've ever endured. At last, the blacksmith released his hand from the electrical wire and stopped the dreadful punishment. I wrenched my hand away from the farmer next to me, cussed him out with the foulest language I'd learned from my friends, then kicked him in his butt with my bare foot. I ran away as fast as my feet could carry me.

The village blacksmith was happy upon seeing that his little test had worked so magnificently. I still recall his snide chuckle while observing our discomfort. The penned horses and cows soon learned to respect the electrified fence, as did the rest of the villagers.

Every now and then, my foster parents welcomed visitors to their home and if they had children, Aunt Sigrid would suggest that I show them around. I usually took them to the creamery, and we often ended up playing in my little shack. If they were interested in animals, I would show them the barns and the farm creatures. If they had never seen an electric fence, then I couldn't wait to show them. Standing next to the electric wire, I dared them to touch it. Most of the time they turned me down. But, on occasion, one of them would grab the shiny wire and get a walloping jolt. It was always so sadistically humorous to watch their astonished reactions.

The Chamberpot

One sunny afternoon Sven saddled up a docile mare named Fia and lifted me onto the saddle. The horse seemed huge to me. Sitting on the saddle, it was a long way down to the ground. Sven led her around the barnyard with me sitting on her broad back. At first, I was scared but I soon gained confidence as little by little I learned how to handle the reins. Every now and then I had a chance to ride on horseback around the village, and my newly found freedom was exciting. Since I was too small to handle the heavy saddle by myself, Sven helped me when he wasn't too busy with his chores, and Fia soon became my horse. I fed and groomed her, and we became good friends. She loved eating carrots and whenever I went to visit her in the barn, I always brought goodies. Sugar cubes were her favorite.

One day Sven asked me if I would like to take Fia, who was hitched to a flatbed wagon, and deliver the village mail to the railroad station. I had turned eight years old that February and Sven thought it might be about time that I took on that responsibility. I couldn't believe what he had just told me. Eagerly I accepted the challenge, which meant leaving the village and riding the wagon on the main rural road with its occasional passing cars. I first had to ride up to the agronomer's mansion to pick up the mail pouch, which was secured with a padlock. I then took off for the station. Fia trotted along the bumpy dirt road leading out of the village and we soon entered the main road which was much smoother and harder. The sun was shining, and it was the most beautiful day, one of those special days which make one want to sing or whistle a lively tune. Luckily there was very little traffic, just the occasional car passing by, raising dust into the air. My immediate destination was the Ryningsnäs railroad station, and it was critical to get the mail pouch there on time as our community was served by a local train which, despite the timetables, rarely arrived on time.

After hitching Fia to a post, I proudly carried the mail pouch to the station house, a small white building situated next to the single railroad track. I entered through a narrow door, and wooden benches for the few travelers lined both sides of the waiting room. The ticketing clerk, an older bespectacled man with a receding hairline, sat behind a barred window. I pushed the mail pouch through an opening. The clerk opened the padlock, and as he dumped the mail into an outgoing mail basket, I selected a seat on the bench to await the incoming train. Of course, the train was late, making the wait longer than necessary. And, I hated to wait.

The station door opened and in came a local farmer with a pained look on his face. His jaw was quite swollen, having somehow been dislocated. He was on his way to see the nearest doctor, whose office happened to be in Målilla, a train ride away from Ryningsnäs. The farmer seated himself amongst the others waiting for the train, his injured jaw causing him great discomfort. As he suffered silently, one could see the pain emanating from his expression. I felt sorry for him as I gazed at his contorted face from the corner of my eye.

In a small village such as Ryningsnäs, the sight of this hapless man could provide sufficient talk for a week. But this was not the end of it. About five minutes later, we heard some commotion outside the station house and looking through the window, we saw the strangest sight ever. Approaching the station was this odd couple, one man leading another who had a porcelain chamber pot stuck over his head. The former led the unlucky man by the arm and cautioned him to watch for the two steps leading to the door. We heard him say, "Axel, be careful, don't trip on the front steps!" The embarrassed man replied in the affirmative, his reverberating voice sounding as if it came from a deep cavern. The door slowly opened, and the chamber-potted man stepped into the waiting room. Also on his way to see the doctor, he was led to a seat on the suddenly vacated bench. As he sat down the large pot clunked against the back rest, adding a comedic flair to the situation. We all sat there, silently spellbound, examining this situation with disbelief. The ticket clerk craned his neck through the barred window to peer curiously at the goings-on. A few minutes passed, then we heard a pained whimper arise from the man with the dislocated jaw. He tried to hold back his laughter as it obviously hurt, but the more he tried to suppress it, the worse it got, until he finally burst out with a bellowing howl which echoed throughout the small station house. With tears in his eyes, he laughed and laughed as he gawked at the unfortunate man. To everyone's amazement, his jaw suddenly jumped back into place with a resounding snap. In recognition of his sudden cure, the farmer quickly got a refund for his unused train ticket to Målilla and, with a big grin, hurriedly left the station. No doubt he couldn't wait to tell his friends about his miraculous recovery. The train finally arrived some fifteen minutes late, but it was the most entertaining fifteen minutes ever experienced by any of us, apart from the pot-headed mystery man. The real story behind the chamber pot never surfaced, but there were some theories kicked around by community members. Perhaps his doctor found out how he managed to stuff his cranium into such an unusual vessel but of course, that's a doctor-client privilege. At any rate, he ain't telling. The ticket clerk filled my mail pouch with the incoming mail, put the padlock in place, and slid it through the ticket window. I picked it up proudly, unhitched Fia, and rode the wagon back to the village. I couldn't wait to tell everyone about the happenings at the Ryningsnäs train station.

Work and Love

During the summertime some twenty university students came to Ryningsnäs to work in the fields. They were undergraduates from Uppsala University, just north of Stockholm. The young college boys were put into the fields to cut the hay, raking it into large piles for air drying, from where it was gathered and loaded onto hay wagons for transport to the haylofts. They worked long hours each day, earning money to pay for their education. Their appetites were enormous, fueled by working the fields under the hot summer sun. The university provided a cook to prepare meals for the young men, and local farmers provided lodging at their homes.

The ground level accommodations of our building were vacant except for the storeroom used for aging the cheese made by Uncle Pelle. The university leased this room to serve as a kitchen and cafeteria for the young student workers. A robust middle-aged woman served as their cook. She began her workday at the crack of dawn preparing food for the hungry farmhands. It took a while to light the wood-fired stove. Once the stove heated up, she hurriedly fixed breakfast for the students who arrived half-asleep, stumbling over each other while taking their seats around three long tables. The loud noises coming from the eatery directly below our kitchen awakened me way before my normal time, but I soon became accustomed to their revelry and horseplay. After wolfing down their breakfasts they departed for their field assignments while the cook, with the help of her fourteen-year-old daughter, cleaned up the now vacant tables.

The cook's daughter, a cute, blue-eyed blonde, was named Gunilla. She was helpful and worked side by side with her mother, clearing the tables and filling large basins with water fetched from the outside pump. She also washed the dishes and helped her mother prepare for the next meal by paring potatoes and carrots. When not working in the kitchen she sat outside and sometimes read books. At first, she seemed shy and kept to herself, but little by little she became talkative and friendly. The afternoons were hers to do with as she pleased. I ran into her many times a day and we soon became friends and went for walks around the village. Her willingness to come with me on these walks made me feel grown-up. Gunilla was vivacious and a lot of fun despite being six years older than I. She was fascinated to see how the cows were milked by machine and she marveled at how many there were. Coming from Stockholm, she had never ventured onto a farm, so she was intrigued with everything I showed her and gladly accompanied me to take in new sights and sounds. She seemed like a sister, and I found it exciting to spend my spare time in her company.

One day we decided to walk along the Em River, starting from our village where the wide river flowed lazily by. It narrowed as we neared the railroad station, and the current became swifter. I decided to show Gunilla the powerhouse and the flour mill. Uncle Pelle had brought me here before when we toured the premises during one of our shopping trips to the village grocery store and since I knew my way around, I proudly brought Gunilla here. The powerhouse was situated where the swift-moving river turned a massive water turbine with a deafening roar. It was connected to a large generator which provided electricity to Ryningsnäs and the surrounding countryside. High transmission power lines which disappeared into the distance got their start here. We toured the powerhouse first and because it was nearly impossible to speak due to the noise, we resorted to shouting and hand-waving. Gunilla seemed overwhelmed by the clamor and followed me cautiously, step by step. I led her by the hand during our walk through the building and she looked at the rotating machinery with great interest.

I then showed her the mill where the local farmers brought their wheat to be ground into flour. Mill workers were busy filling burlap sacks with the flour and the air was filled with dust particles which made breathing difficult. The river provided power to turn the millstones as well. I had always been intrigued by machinery of all sorts and I don't know how Gunilla felt about it, but she did show enthusiasm for our little tour.

It was time to get back to the village, so we returned along the river where it again slowed to a crawl. The farmers used the river for recreation as well as for bathing. I had been forbidden to go near the river by myself since I hadn't yet learned to swim because Aunt Sigrid and Uncle Pelle were always too busy to teach me. Gunilla, on the other hand, was a strong swimmer, and before returning to the creamery she said that she wanted to take a swim in the river. Before I realized it, she disappeared behind a bush. To my pleasant surprise, she reappeared in the nude and jumped into the river. She waved at me from the cool water and coaxed me to join her, but I remained on the shore watching with pleasure as she demonstrated her breaststroke and backstroke. She wasn't at all modest. This was my first experience seeing a naked girl. During our walk home I was secretly hoping to see her without her clothes again. She stirred unusual feelings inside me which I had never experienced before. I kept looking at her as if seeing her for the first time. I liked and respected her, being older than I and so sure of herself. And she was so pretty. Dinnertime was rapidly approaching, and she was needed by her mother to help prepare supper for the returning student laborers. I hoped to spend more time with her the following day.

Weeks passed. I worked in the fields, weeding and thinning vegetable crops. It was still hard work, though I had become used to the drudgery. My knees were callused as well as my hands. I was able to thin four rows in one day which made the walk home a little shorter, so I settled on this pace and didn't try to improve upon it. When I got home, I finally had a chance to see Gunilla again. We went to pick wildflowers which grew along the seldom traveled roads near the farm. While picking long-stemmed yellow and blue flowers, I taught Gunilla how to make a crown for herself by lacing them together. Aunt Sigrid had taught me how during one of our Sunday outings. The multicolored flowers looked terrific with Gunilla's blonde hair. We talked about her home in Stockholm and how much fun she had living in Sweden's capital. I hoped to see more of Stockholm someday. I told her about seeing the tall, brick city hall building, with its three golden crowns adorning the towers, and the palace of the King of Sweden, which was an imposing structure. Gunilla's father had deserted the family a few years earlier, so she lived with just her mother and had no sisters or brothers. She had not looked forward to coming to Ryningsnäs, but with each day she grew more and more fond of our little village and its country life. As we talked, we picked more flowers, enough to fill several vases.

We brought the flowers back home and arranged them in empty milk bottles. There were enough flowers to adorn the tabletops in the cafeteria. I brought one flower-filled bottle upstairs and set it quietly on the kitchen table, careful not to wake my napping foster parents. Then I raced downstairs to meet Gunilla and suggested we go into the dairy to cool off since it was a sweltering day. The dairy was closed for the rest of the afternoon, and it was quiet, the tile floors still wet from the cleanup. I picked up the water hose and asked I could cool her off, secretly hoping to see her in the nude once again. Turning on the water, I directed the spray on her bare feet. Not wanting to get her dress wet, she quickly disrobed. I remained speechless seeing her naked and found it hard to swallow. My secret wish had suddenly become a reality. The water sprayed on her bare body as she stood there, first facing me and then turning her back. I was fascinated seeing her lithe body as she giggled and danced around and around. Her hair was wet as she smiled at me and she didn't seem the least bit shy as my eyes wandered over her smooth body. I kept swallowing over and over, feeling very strange.

After a while she came over to me and snatched the hose from my hands, telling me that it was my turn to be showered down. I was quite embarrassed but, then again, I felt the urge to quickly remove my pants. Facing away from her, I yanked them off, and now we were both naked as jay birds. What a wonderful feeling. She aimed the cool water on my backside, starting from my shoulders then slowly lowering the stream all the way down to my ankles. No longer ashamed, I stood there enjoying the cool spray of the water. The incredible feeling was a new awakening. My heart was beating furiously as she continued to hose me down and I agonized that someone might walk in and find us here, which added to the excitement. Just imagine what Uncle Pelle or Aunt Sigrid would have said. How would I ever explain my way out of this one? After cooling down in this most pleasing way we reluctantly dressed and I felt great relief that we had not been discovered. I hoped we would do it again sometime to see what might happen next, as my curiosity had been awakened. The fond memories of that sultry afternoon in the Ryningsnäs dairy would stay with me for a long time.

Out In Nature

The summer days were warm and wonderful. I used to go for short walks in the meadows and woods and on one beautiful day, after returning home from school, I changed into my trunks and headed out. Aunt Sigrid and Uncle Pelle were taking their customary naps after a grueling day in the creamery and my supper was sitting on the kitchen table as usual. After eating my meal, I left the house and walked over to a nearby meadow. The grassy fields led to a small hill and there were no houses in the vicinity. The meadow flowers were in full bloom and the air was still except for the chirping birds. This was one of my favorite places when I wanted to be alone.

I had come here for a specific purpose and was excited about what I was planning to do. Finding no one around, I crossed the meadow, slowly pulling at the edges of my trunks, lowering them inch by inch. As I continued my walk, my trunks drifted slowly to the ground, leaving me completely naked. It was a wonderful feeling being here all alone, though I kept looking around to make sure that no one saw me. There was always the element of fear, of being found out, which made it that much more exciting.

I left my trunks behind a rock and walked a short distance away. The slight wind caressed my naked body. Gaining more confidence, I walked a little further away each time, increasing the chance of being discovered. My excitement grew more with each step. I climbed up to the top of a small hill in total nakedness. There were little trees here and there which could provide some cover should a passerby come along the country road. I could see the road from bend to bend and affirmed that there was no one around. Nakedness gave me a feeling of complete freedom, so I continued my nature walk.

Suddenly, the thought of not being able to find my hidden shorts popped into my mind, so, turning back, I carefully retraced my steps. I looked behind several rocks but could not find them, which concerned me as I wondered how I would ever get home. How could I possibly explain this situation? It would be a great embarrassment, not only for me but also for my foster parents. No longer enjoying myself, I continued the search. The thought of someone finding and stealing them crossed my mind. At last, I managed to locate them, and, with a sigh of relief, I slipped them on, hoping to return here another day. I returned to this favorite spot every now and then, each time becoming more daring with my secret pleasure. Nudism has its virtues and can be a way of life for some. For me, it was a part of growing up.

Little Entrepeneur

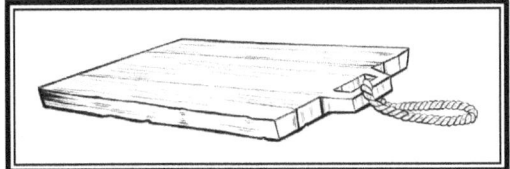

I loved the smell of fresh sawdust. The scrap pile, left behind by the sawyer, contained some odd lengths of birch, pine and oak. One day I found a wonderful use for them. Using Uncle Pelle's hand saw, I cut all the blocks to the same length and after sanding down the rough edges I built cutting boards from these scraps. My foster parents had given me a wood carving set as a birthday present and it was time to learn how to use it. I carved various flower shapes and butterflies into my boards. I presented my first piece to Aunt Sigrid, and she was so pleased that she encouraged me to make more of them to sell to the neighbors. The work was painstakingly slow but with each board the job became faster and easier. I found shortcuts here and there and the quality improved. I set up a little table at the dairy's loading dock and when the farmers brought their filled milk cans for processing, I showed them my pieces of art and managed to sell a few each week. The villagers eventually decided that I wasn't quite the delinquent kid despite having burnt down the forest. Uncle Pelle added my newly earned income to the growing stash of money gained from working in the fields each summer.

Tutte happened by one day to play. I told him that I was busy building these cutting boards and that I had earned some extra money in the process. He gave them a cursory examination and because I couldn't play, he left in a huff. Tutte related the story to his older brother Roland, and after hearing about my successful sales, they decided to compete with me. They got busy making cutting boards on their own, dreaming about making some easy money. Their work, as I found out later, was shoddy at best. In lieu of painstakingly sanding their boards, they left the surfaces rough, and rather than carving the designs, they drew them on instead. Of course, when the boards got wet the ink ran all over, obliterating the design. Their sales were even more dismal: after peddling their product from door to door they found no buyers at all. Aunt Sigrid, having spoken to one of the neighbors, related their failed sales campaign to me. I tried to keep from laughing but soon Aunt Sigrid and I had a good guffaw.

Tutte and Roland were crushed following this humiliating experience. Not only were they angry with me but they were also jealous and wouldn't talk to me for days. But one day, Tutte, seemingly in a good mood, came by to give me a small gift which he'd wrapped in newspaper and tied with some baggage string. He told me not to open it until the following day and to hide it from Sigrid and Pelle, suggesting that I put it under my bed. I was a bit surprised by this sudden show of generosity, considering our recent spat, so bringing it upstairs I slid it under my bed. After falling asleep in my cozy bed, I suddenly woke up in the middle of the night to a disgusting smell. Recognizing the odor, I thought that I might have soiled the bed, but it was spotless and so was I.

What in the world was going on? I looked around trying to find the source of the obnoxious stench, then remembered Tutte's package under my bed. I cautiously opened it and held my breath. There was one of Tutte's rejected cutting boards, the top smeared with his gooey excrement. This was utterly disgusting! I couldn't believe he did this to me. I wrapped it up quickly and, holding my breath, snuck out of the building and headed for the outhouse. Now it dawned on me why Tutte had told me not to open it until the next day. It was a nasty revenge.

After tossing the "gift" through the outhouse hole, I pushed it deeper into the pile of feces with the crap-poker. Reassuring myself that it was totally hidden, I started to plan a counter-offensive. How could I possibly top this dastardly act? I was quite certain that it was all Roland's idea. Angrily I walked back to the house, went to bed and let my mind ponder a suitable retribution. Fortunately, Uncle Pelle and Aunt Sigrid were totally unaware of the circumstances. I felt ashamed having been treated so poorly and didn't want anyone to ever learn about it.

I woke up the next morning with a great plan, but first I had to tend to my daily chores. I replenished the water bucket and the firewood pile and then swatted the small swarm of flies with a well-worn fly swatter. When I finally saw Tutte and Roland that afternoon I thanked them politely for their gift. I tried my best to remain calm and collected, never letting on what I had experienced earlier. Not a word, no angry remarks. Tutte and Roland stood there speechless, waiting for an outburst which never came. I knew then that my revenge was working. They were dying to see my expression of anger and disgust and instead found me congenial, with a big smile on my face. Tutte, no longer able to contain himself, finally queried my thoughts regarding his package. Expecting an outburst, they were once again disappointed to see a broad smile instead. The hollow, incredulous look on their faces gave me the utmost satisfaction. I had succeeded with my own brand of vengeance. I asked Tutte if he wanted to go to the schoolyard to play, but he was in no mood to accompany me there. Instead, Tutte and Roland slowly shuffled homeward with their tails between their legs. Rejoicing in my subtle victory, I watched them depart. After all, who would they tell?

Film-Making

Always interested in new things, I moved on to another project: making movies. (I developed an interest in movies when my mother took me to see my very first film, Snow White and the Seven Dwarves.) I went to the boiler room in the creamery and played with some old lenses, trying to make a movie projector. I had a strong flashlight, some old negatives, and a white box which served as a screen. I tried to focus the lens in such a way as to project the image of the negative on the little screen. Armed with lenses from old flashlights, I fashioned a long tube out of cardboard and tried projecting a picture on the wall. I found that I had to hold the negative upside-down for it to be projected right-side-up on the screen. I spent many a day down there experimenting, and Uncle Pelle joined me from time to time. I made some progress, but I just didn't have the right kind of lights and lenses to get anywhere.

To my great surprise, Uncle Pelle and Aunt Sigrid got me an honest-to-goodness movie projector for Christmas. It was hand-operated with a little crank and a regular-sized light bulb inside. I also got a roll of film which, when cranked through the projector, presented a home movie of people around a picnic table in someone's home in Sweden, though, lacking a story line, we quickly tired of watching. Since there was no take-up spool for the film, it gathered on the floor in a huge pile and had to be rolled up by hand. But the movie machine was mine to keep. Luckily for us, the film never caught on fire, though it was extremely flammable. I knew that I would have a great use for it once I returned to Finland, equipped with my spyglass which Uncle Pelle now had under lock and key.

End of Long Life

Word spread that Mr. Johnson suddenly passed away. It had become more difficult for Mrs. Johnson, now in her mid-seventies, to care for him after a stroke left him partially paralyzed. The neighbors pitched in on a regular basis, helping them with their daily chores, though Mrs. Johnson was still capable of preparing the meals and tending to her husband's needs. Their home, which had fortunately escaped the forest fire caused by the careless use of my spyglass, was located near the creamery along the village road. Parts of the forest remained scarred, but new growth of foliage could already be seen.

I had visited the Johnsons on several occasions prior to Mr. Johnson's stroke. He was a retired sea captain who was full of exciting stories about his life on the high seas at the helm of a majestic sailing ship. Spellbound, I listened to his stories even though at times he retold the same ones, having become a little forgetful. One of his prized possessions was a miniature sailing ship inside a clear glass bottle. Mr. Johnson built it himself years before and the workmanship was simply superb. Each sail and its rigging were accurately placed. It must have been a painstaking accomplishment.

He had assembled the ship with its sails laying on top of the boat, then slipped it inside the bottle through its small opening. The sails had been carefully hoisted with the aid of a long string left hanging from the bottle's mouth. On the bottle's label was a painting of Captain Johnson at the helm of a sailing ship which listed dangerously amid a stormy sea.

Following the fire, I had been reluctant to pay the Johnsons a visit as I feared a severe tongue-lashing. But my fears had been unfounded. When Aunt Sigrid insisted that I bring them some spring flowers earlier that year, Mr. and Mrs. Johnson gracefully accepted them in an offering of forgiveness.

On hearing of his passing, Aunt Sigrid was among the neighbors who came to help Mrs. Johnson. Her husband died peacefully in the early morning hours, still seated in his rocking chair. Mrs. Johnson summoned Tutte's mother and shared the sad news. Other neighbors joined in to lend a helping hand. I asked Aunt Sigrid if I could come with her, never having seen a dead person and being morbidly curious. She reluctantly agreed, provided I stay out of everyone's way.

The wood stove was fired up promptly and before long the strong scent of coffee drifted throughout the little house. The traditional Swedish cream puffs, brought by a neighbor, made their way to the table. It was customary to dunk them into your coffee cup and enjoy them with slurping sounds. Even the kids loved coffee and it was commonly served to us. A lot of coffee was to be consumed on this day. Mrs. Johnson kept saying over and over that she would have to consult with her husband about the arrangements, not registering that he was gone for eternity. She sobbed and clenched her hands. Captain Johnson's corpse was still seated on the rocking chair. His eyes were closed, and he seemed fast asleep. I was told to leave the house and stay outside, but curiosity caused me to sneak back in and watch the proceedings from a distance. I was careful not to get in anyone's way.

The embalming process was unheard-of in the countryside, making it necessary to bury the deceased as soon as possible to prevent spoilage. The long kitchen table was cleared and readied for the corpse. Mr. Johnson's stiffened body was lugged from the rocking chair into the kitchen, where it required four people to lift him onto the table. Now the real problem had begun, as rigor mortis had set in. Why, Mr. Johnson was the stiffest thing in town that morning. It took the efforts of all the women to straighten him out. When the upper body was pushed down on the table the legs went up in the air, and when attempting to push the legs down, the torso raised up. It seemed cruelly hilarious to watch the teetering stiff rocking up and down on the table. After considerable effort of stretching and pulling, Mr. Johnson was finally straightened into a prone position. The flies had also found him, swirling around and lighting mercilessly on his body. Mrs. Johnson, still confused and bereaved, kept asking Mr. Johnson's preference regarding a choice of suits for the burial. Of course, Mr. Johnson remained without comment; he probably didn't care at all. It was going to take a few days for Mrs. Johnson to realize that her husband had really died.

Mr. Johnson was about to be undressed and fitted with his captain's uniform. Adding to the difficulties, the corpse had dirtied its pants. I took the liberty of stepping outside into the fresh air, as the Johnson's kitchen was definitely not the place to be. Once decked out in his naval uniform, Captain Johnson was placed into a crude wooden coffin and carried outside to a nearby shed. Blocks of ice from the creamery were placed on and around the coffin to preserve the body until burial.

Early Sunday morning the coffin was loaded onto a horse-drawn wagon and transported to the cemetery in Målilla. I didn't have to go, thank goodness. I guessed that the velvet-handed minister would tend to his duties and talk with God, thus assuring Mr. Johnson a safe passage to the next world. The death of Mr. Johnson seemed to finally dawn on the black-clad Mrs. Johnson, as I never ever heard her talk to him again.

Life Cut Short

Once on a beautiful summer's day I got a day off from field work. School was closed and the leisure time was mine. I decided to pay a visit to Jan, the orchard keeper, and talk him out of some fresh fruit right off the tree. The orchard was on the back side of the agronomer's mansion, and had rows of apple trees, two kinds of pear trees, and red and yellow cherry trees, my very favorite. Cherries picked directly from the tree were the sweetest of all. Jan had given me an open invitation to select a few pieces of fruit every now and then, so that's where I was headed.

Jan was a soft-spoken, friendly guy with a perpetual smile. His wife, Hilma, the mother of their only child named Karl, spent her time as a housewife. She loved her five-year-old son with all her heart; he was the apple of her eye. Karl liked watching his father as he worked in the orchard, pruning tree branches and weeding the gardens. Sometimes Karl got in the way of falling tree branches and was sent home to his mother. Today was such a day, and arriving home to find his mother, Hilma, busy preparing lunch for the family, Karl decided to play with the family kitten which they had found wandering through the orchard and adopted.

After filling a basket with assorted cherries, I thanked Jan and returned home. Uncle Pelle and Aunt Sigrid had just finished closing the creamery for the day and were readying for their afternoon nap. After eating my meal in solitude, it was time to enjoy some of the cherries, which were plump, ripe, and oh so wonderful. I made sure to save some so that Uncle Pelle and Aunt Sigrid could enjoy them as well after waking from their nap.

About five o'clock that afternoon, a neighbor came running over to our house asking for Uncle Pelle and Aunt Sigrid. Reluctantly, I awakened them from their slumber, and they got up, still groggy from their nap. The breathless neighbor stepped into the kitchen to inform my parents that Karl was missing. Quickly slipping on their clogs, they joined the search party being organized in the village.

Jan had returned home after finishing his work in the orchard and saw the alarmed look on his wife's face. Hilma had been looking everywhere for little Karl and together the two searched the surrounding area. When their search proved fruitless, Jan summoned his neighbor to help. It didn't take long before the news of Karl's disappearance reached the rest of the nearby villagers, and they quickly organized a search party. Hilma had last seen Karl playing with their kitten, but he had apparently gone back outside and wandered off. She finished preparing his lunch and after calling for him to come in to eat, found that he was missing.

The search party split into groups of three and looked in different areas. They searched the orchard, the surrounding fields, the barnyard, and the numerous farm buildings; they checked every nook and cranny. Whenever one of their own needed help, the villagers never hesitated. The search for Karl continued through the late afternoon, and luckily, the summer days remained light until late. The agronomer joined the search with his hunting dog. He had been provided with some of the boy's clothing to get his scent and the dog, with nose to the ground, pulled heavily on his leash. After removing the leash, the dog excitedly sniffed around. At times he seemed to have lost the scent but then, picking it up again, he headed toward the Em River. The agronomer followed the dog with Jan a few steps behind. As the dog neared the river the anxiety level of the villagers reached a fever pitch. Jan feared the worst. Suddenly the dog ducked into the midst of a thicket of bushes by the river's edge. The embankment was steep and hard to penetrate, but the orchard keeper pushed his way through the bushes, following the dog. His heart was pounding, and his face was flushed as he disappeared into the thicket and reached the swiftly flowing river. Stepping into the water up to his waist, he slowly waded downstream holding onto the underbrush. The dog had ended his search at the river's edge and Jan worked his way along the bank, fervently hoping that Karl wouldn't be found there. Down the river he waded, constantly calling out his son's name. Other searchers had joined in farther downstream. Startled birds shot out from the thicket, squawking with fright.

Suddenly a long, wailing cry came from the river's edge. That heart wrenching cry spoke volumes. Trapped in some low-hanging branches, Jan had found the lifeless body of his son whose little body was blue and scratched from scraping against the low-hanging branches. Crying with tormented anguish, Jan carefully freed his son from the vegetation and the slow-moving river. He cradled him as he cried out in pain. The agronomer helped him up the steep riverbank with tear-filled eyes. By now, more villagers had reached the riverbank. Their mood was somber; no one had expected the search to end this way.

Clearing the thicket to even ground, Jan carried the lifeless body of his beloved son. He was suffering from shock which made it difficult to walk. His friends helped him slowly back to his home, and not a word was spoken, save low whispers from the villagers. Their spirits were dampened, and many cried silently, mourning the loss of Karl. Hilma was devastated upon seeing her son's body. Blaming herself over and over, she couldn't accept the fact of her loss. "How could this have happened?" she moaned repeatedly. Jan felt so very guilty having gruffly sent his son home lest he be injured by a falling tree branch during his pruning. If he could only bring back the earlier time of day. If, if, if! But the stark reality of the day prevailed. Friends and neighbors tried to comfort the sorrowful parents. but they couldn't ease their pain. Little Karl was laid to rest in Målilla, where the soft-handed minister performed a beautiful funeral sermon. The unexpected loss of their son would dwell in the hearts of his loving parents, as well as those of the villagers. Somehow, however, life would go on amidst this unforeseeable sadness.

A Wedding and a Romp in the Hay

Weddings in Ryningsnäs were special events. I had a chance to attend a wedding and the ensuing celebration of a happy bride and groom who were in their mid-twenties. The parents of the groom owned a stately mansion nearby, and their home was the second largest in the immediate area. It was a two-story house built in the shade of old oak trees and was surrounded by well-groomed lawns with a gravel driveway leading to the guest entrance. The invited guests would arrive in their horse drawn carriages.

My Finnish friend Rolf was being fostered by the groom's family. He was lucky to be living in this splendid home. By comparison, my home seemed spartan. But I never envied Rolf his good fortune as his life was not all fun and games. He worked hard and his workday ended after sundown. Rolf was quite a bit bigger and stronger than me, and he was a born leader with a devilish streak. He never missed an opportunity to cook up some excitement for the village kids, and tonight would be no exception.

The wedding preparations had gone on for several

weeks. The guest list included most of the surrounding families and villagers, including my foster parents and me. The minister from Målilla was invited to perform the wedding. The front yard had been manicured to perfection. One of the most interesting wedding customs in Sweden involved the downing of a large birch tree from which a fine piece of furniture would be crafted for the newly married couple's home. The appointed tree had long been selected by the village cabinetmaker who had spent several days in search of the perfect birch. Finding one to his satisfaction, it was carefully marked and saved for this special event. A tree-cutting party formed to fell the tree and drag it from the forest to the wedding site. If the tree happened to be a large one, it required many strong-backed men to accomplish the task.

The time came for the selected party revelers to head to the forest and the cabinetmaker led his group of merry men to the stately birch tree. There they stood, surrounding it and taking long swigs of aquavit, a Swedish version of vodka. Once the bottle was consumed another quickly took its place. Before long, the men were singing in unison, getting ready for the tree felling. Even Tutte's father had found his way here, uninvited of course. No one seemed to notice his presence, no doubt desensitized by the effects of the aquavit. Two men cut into the virgin tree with a large saw which caused sap to ooze from the open wound. Back and forth the saw blade moved, cutting ever deeper into the trunk. The tall tree shuddered for a moment, and leaning very slowly, began its mortal fall. Having been warned several times, the kids stood a safe distance away from the falling tree. Obeying our elders, we watched the majestic birch fall to the ground. Its branches swept against nearby trees as it gained momentum. When it hit the ground with a resounding crash, it raised the dust into a whirlwind, sending leaves flying high into the air.

There was an eerie calm followed by a loud cheer from the tipsy merrymakers. Then, a soft wailing sound emanated from the surrounding brush, followed by strong cuss words. Rushing toward the sounds, the tree cutters found, much to their surprise, none other than Tutte's uninvited father, who had earned the name of Village Idiot, brought about by his reckless lifestyle. There he lay, crumpled under a large tree branch. He had taken quite a hit. Luckily the trunk had missed him, preventing certain death. A branch pinned him to the forest floor and rested on his left leg. He was grimacing with pain and cussing all the while. It took several villagers to lift the branch and a couple of others to pull him free of the tree. I swear I heard someone mutter, "He had it coming, the stupid shit." Too far away to be seen by the doctor in Målilla, he was anesthetized with several, long pulls from the aquavit bottle and hoisted on top of the birch tree next to a sturdy branch. The fiery alcohol soon consoled the man and he found comfort nesting in the fallen tree.

The second phase was about to get underway. The singing revelers lined up on both sides of the large birch and, groaning loudly, began pulling it out of the forest. With great effort they inched their prize from the woods onto the dirt road. This was some sight. Only in rural Sweden! The adrenaline-charged men soon found a marching tempo between dragging the tree and taking swigs of aquavit. The wedding party was about to begin just as the prone tree appeared in the front yard. Tutte's dad, oblivious to the surroundings, sang drunkenly as he lay in the crotch of the tree branches. His sudden appearance raised a lot of curious eyebrows as he was carried into the house and placed on a wooden bench. A makeshift splint was attached to the broken leg to keep it immobile. Luckily, he was no longer in pain; the aquavit had done its job.

The huge tree had been hauled to the side of the house and the branches would be cut off in the days to come. The gifted cabinetmaker would have the tree milled into smooth boards, being sure to use them all to build beautiful pieces of furniture. The finished pieces would be presented to the newlywed couple as wedding gifts from the villagers. What a wonderful custom.

A visiting minister from Målilla performed the wedding in the garden. No sooner was the knot tied than the festivities began. Long tables set up in nearby fields were filled with delicacies brought out by dozens of servants. The hungry guests filled the benches and tables with overloaded plates. Others sat on the grassy lawns and on the front steps leading to the decorated house. There was more food than one could ever imagine: fresh pork hams, fried chicken, and Swedish meatballs adorned the serving tables while freshly picked country vegetables rounded out the servings. Dark, delicious breads and newly churned butter were there for the choosing, and jugs of delicious mead were served in tin cups. We devoured the feast with voracious appetites. Swedish pastries and hot coffee followed the meal. Of course, I dug in, taking several cream puffs which Aunt Sigrid was usually too tired to make following her long workdays.

The crowd found their places around the blazing bonfire. More tin cups filled with spiked punch were passed to the celebrants. Local musicians had gathered near the fire and began playing waltzes and polkas. The happy attendees eagerly watched the dancing newlywed couple with smiles on their faces. Others joined in dancing to the lively and familiar tunes. The punchbowls were filled repeatedly during the evening, and Rolf kept us kids supplied with the tasty mead. No one was paying attention to us as we emptied cup after cup of the intoxicating beverage. We had so much fun all evening and the party continued late into the night. When we finally tired from the revelry, Rolf led us to the barn, and we climbed up into the hayloft. Burrowing into the hay, we listened to the sounds of music and merrymaking.

I must have drifted off in a deep sleep, but sometime during the night I was awakened by strange sounds. At first, I couldn't remember where I was, though it finally dawned on me that I was still in the hayloft. The night was quiet; the music had stopped, and people had either drifted home or spent the night in the large mansion. The hayloft was dark except for a few stray moonbeams peeking through cracks in the ceiling. As I lay there, quietly, listening for more sounds, I realized that we kids had been joined by others. Unaware of my presence, a young couple lay a few feet away. I spotted a bare buttock bobbing up and down between a pair of upturned legs, then heard more of the unfamiliar sounds which had awakened me. I didn't really understand what was going on and was a bit afraid that he was hurting her in some way. I held my breath, not wanting to be discovered. Then the bobbing increased in tempo as their breathing reached fever pitch. I even heard a muffled scream, followed by total silence. I was totally dumbfounded but decided to try to go back to sleep. *Then*, someone threw up. That sound I had heard many times. The retching noises lasted for quite some time. I caught a whiff of the repulsive odor of vomit, and, having had more than my share of the mead, my stomach became uneasy. This proved to be too much, and I had to get out of there. While digging myself out from my cozy nest of hay I almost stepped on the couple next to me. The girl suddenly screamed in stark horror and her boyfriend cussed loudly at me. Before they could grab me, I was out of there in a flash. Rolf was also wide awake and joined me as we scrambled out of the barn into the fresh air.

Dawn lit up the morning sky as roosters began crowing. I couldn't wait to tell Rolf what I had witnessed in the barn. He laughed at me and let me in on a secret: "Just like the stallion and the mare," he chuckled, "Just like the stallion and the mare." I was shocked. I simply didn't know that people did that too.

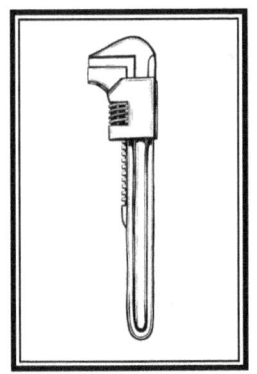

The Boiler Caper

Uncle Pelle woke me early one morning and I was startled to see him standing there with his pungent smelling kerosene lantern. He told me that the electricity had gone out in the entire village, so the time had come to start up the steam engine in the boiler room. Knowing of my keen interest in machinery and my many questions about the steam engine, he knew that I would gladly get up to watch him. A major fire of unknown origin had damaged the main power-generating station as well as the flour mill. It had occurred late in the evening and now we were all without electricity. The agronomer's cows had to be milked by hand and, being an exhausting task, additional workers were summoned to get the job done. Failure to do so would result in injury to the large herd of milking cows, which had to be prevented at all costs.

Uncle Pelle and I entered the boiler room. He stoked the large oven at the bottom of the boiler with newspaper and firewood. Before long the fire was crackling noisily. The boiler, fed by the reservoir, was always kept full of water for such emergencies. Checking the numerous gauges and dials,

Uncle Pelle waited for the water temperature to reach boiling, then, by opening certain valves, the steam was directed to the engine. It resembled a steam locomotive in that it had a steam cylinder, piston, connecting rod, and a slider crank mechanism. The slider crank was connected to a massive flywheel about five feet in diameter. With steam hissing, the piston sprang into action and pushed the slider crank forward, slowly at first, barely turning the flywheel. With each succeeding stroke the flywheel began to rotate faster and faster, turning the entire room into a noisy wonderland. I was fascinated by the sights and sounds. Uncle Pelle scampered from the boiler to the steam engine and back, continuously peering at the various gauges, ascertaining the safe operation of his equipment.

The flywheel's speed was checked by a strange looking contraption called a speed governor which consisted of a vertical shaft geared to the flywheel. Two round steel balls rotated around the shaft. As the speed of rotation increased, the balls swung outward and upward. When the rotating balls reached a certain height, they controlled the steam flow to the cylinder, preventing the steam engine from reaching excessive speeds. A runaway steam engine could cause a catastrophic accident, thus the speed governor assured safe operation of the machine. Taking a few seconds every now and then, Uncle Pelle explained the workings of the emergency equipment. He then proudly answered all my questions. This was surely more interesting than looking at his many scars.

The time had come to start the machinery in the adjoining creamery. A long driveshaft extending from the motor room spanned the creamery and the boiler room.

At first, Uncle Pelle disconnected the drive belt to the now defunct electric motor, then he connected the main driveshaft to the steam engine flywheel. Numerous pulleys attached to the main driveshaft were fitted with belt drives to operate the pasteurizer, the cream separator, the butter churn, the auxiliary generator, and a multitude of pumps used to move the milk. Electricity was restored and the creamery was once again back in business. Lines of wagons lined up along the loading dock brought the raw milk to be processed. The long workday had begun.

It would take the better part of a month to repair the main generator at the flourmill during which time Ryningsnäs would be lit by carbide and kerosene lights as well as candles. Even the agronomer was forced to use them. The long summer evenings were ever so welcome.

The farmers bringing their milk to the dairy talked about the mill fire and wondered what had caused it. Was it arson? An act of God? There was much speculation. I didn't care one way or another as we now had electricity and I was in seventh heaven after witnessing the start-up of the steam engine, and I got to watch it run every day. My foster parents provided continuous service to the community which made their working day even longer: extra tasks now included lighting the boiler, cutting additional firewood, dumping ashes, and careful maintenance of the steam engine. Only Uncle Pelle was able to decipher the readings on the gauges and the operation of the various faucets. Several weeks went by during the repair of the village generating station.

The dairy continued its operation until the old boiler broke down. The steam pressure had been dropping all day long and Uncle Pelle suspected a leak in the boiler. It had to be repaired at once. After it cooled to a safe temperature, Uncle Pelle decided to tackle the job. I asked him if I could watch and maybe even help. He dragged out a long ladder and worked his way up to the top of the still-warm tank. Opening the water valves, he quickly drained the vessel, then one by one removed the bolts from the access cover on top. Warm air seeped out from the cavernous hole. The interior of the tank was filled with a maze of pipes.

While Uncle Pelle was prying the cover off, he accidentally dropped his monkey wrench into the tank. It was beyond his reach and the opening was too small for him. Though he could see the wrench, he had no means of recovering it. "Matti," he said, "Climb the ladder and see if you can reach it." As I stood near the top rung, side by side with Uncle Pelle, we peered into the darkness illuminated only by his flashlight. The hot, humid air wafted from the boiler opening, fogging up my glasses. It had a foul, oily smell. The steam pipes were roughly a foot below the tank opening. He asked me if I would consider climbing through the hole to retrieve his wrench. Would I have the courage and willingness to help him out? Reluctantly, I swung my legs through the opening until I reached the closely spaced piping, then I carefully lowered myself inside the boiler. The interior was still warm to the touch, and it took a while to get used to the darkness. With the aid of the flashlight, I spotted the wrench caught between two pipes, so I lay down on my belly, extended my right arm between the pipes and grabbed ahold of the tool.

When it came time to pull it up, I realized, to my horror, that my wrist was stuck between the piping. I felt a jolt of adrenaline coursing through my body and for a moment, I froze. Panic-stricken, I cried for help. Seeing my predicament, Uncle Pelle told me to drop the wrench and to open my fist to free my arm. I did as I was told, but still unable to extricate my arm, I became scared out of my wits. Sensing the critical situation, Uncle Pelle asked me to remain calm, then told me that he was going to get some butter from the storage locker. Leaving me inside the tank with only the flashlight for comfort, he scurried down the ladder and disappeared into the creamery. His absence seemed eternal, and visions of dying like this entered my mind. I hadn't been so scared since my early childhood when I'd attempted to crawl through hip-deep snow with approaching Russian airplanes dropping their bombs. At last, I could hear Uncle Pelle climbing the ladder. Aunt Sigrid, frightened out of her wits, had accompanied him and was standing on the floor next to the boiler. Uncle Pelle reached down into the opening and placed a chunk of warm butter in my free hand. I couldn't reach my imprisoned wrist, so I spread the gooey stuff on my arm. The melting butter trickled down my arm and found its way to my wrist. My chest was bruised and hurt from lying on the piping, and my steamed-up glasses were cocked to one side making it very difficult to see. I tried wiggling my wrist, which by now had begun to slightly swell. Ignoring the pain, I yanked hard and, finally, managed to free my wrist. With jubilation I got on my knees and raised myself slowly from the boiler. Aunt Sigrid was crying with relief as I climbed down the ladder with Uncle Pelle's help. "But Matti, did you get the wrench?" he asked me with a sly grin. I don't remember answering because Aunt Sigrid really laid into him, uttering words that I had never before heard her say.

Uncle Pelle left the wrench inside the boiler where I dropped it. The village blacksmith came over the next day and made repairs to the boiler, but the creamery remained closed for a couple of days until the repairs were completed. Some of the milk had to be dumped due to lack of room in the chilling tanks. As for Aunt Sigrid's scorching words, well, they would ring in Uncle Pelle's ears for some time to come. I could hardly wait to tell the story to my friends at school.

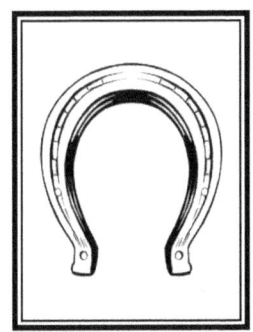

Growing Up

I had become accustomed to my life in Sweden and living with Uncle Pelle and Aunt Sigrid. I no longer missed my life in Finland. My mother, although still in my thoughts, seemed so far away and I found that I didn't miss her very much. "Out of sight, out of mind," I suppose. My foster parents treated me like their own child. Since they had lost their twelve-year-old daughter, my presence filled the loneliness of their grief. They never talked about her with me, though she must have been in their hearts and minds. I was their little boy, at least for a while. Occasionally I would catch glimpses of their sorrow, but for the most part it was well-disguised. Hopefully I brought some comfort to them. I had learned to love them very much. Uncle Pelle filled a void in my life, since I never knew my own dad. I learned so much from him, even though he chastised me from time to time. Uncle Pelle wrote several letters to my mother, which she had translated into Finnish. Occasionally I received a letter from her addressed to the Perssons, but they couldn't understand its contents.

My foster parents worked hard, and their life was totally consumed by the creamery. The cows never took a day off,

127

so all the people involved with them had to keep abreast of these domesticated beasts. Things at the creamery rarely changed. Sundays remained a day of rest and the fresh milk, obtained on Sunday by rotating farm hands, was chilled in the large cooling tanks to be processed on Monday mornings.

My life, on the other hand, continued to vary. School time was a lot of fun, and reaching a higher grade was always a new experience. The field work was left for the summer months, so I found more time to myself in the late fall.

On occasion I visited the blacksmith, Mr. Andersson, while he worked in his shop, and he always welcomed me into his working quarters. He was a clever man capable of making most anything, just short of a magician. He used a forge to make horseshoes out of straight bars of metal, which he put into burning coal embers. He got the fire almost white hot by pumping a giant bellows by hand, and he even let me help him out sometimes by pumping the bellows handle. With a pair of long-handled pliers he pulled the red-hot rod out of the fire and beat the end of it flat. Cutting it into the proper length, he forged the metal into a horseshoe shape. The forging hammer made a lot of noise and sparks flew in all directions. When the shoe was finished, he quenched it by dipping it into a water bath and the hot shoe sizzled and hissed as it cooled. There were boxes of completed horseshoes awaiting delivery to the horse barn.

On our farm was an old tractor with massive iron wheels and only the blacksmith knew how to start the engine, though he had to tinker with it for some time before getting it started. The smell of raw gasoline wafted through the air, reminding me of speeding cars on their way to exciting destinations. The tractor was used extensively to pull various farm implements. The sound of the tractor was often heard from morning till late in the evening. Whenever it broke down, Mr. Andersson was there to repair it.

One time, while riding Aunt Sigrid's bicycle on a narrow path in the woods, I accidentally broke off the pedal when I hit a rock. I had to walk the bike home, fearing a tongue-lashing since she used it frequently to do her errands. Uncle Pelle assured me that Mr. Andersson could fix it in a jiffy. He managed to weld the broken pieces together, thus relieving me of my fears of punishment.

Mr. Andersson once made me a part for my erector set which I had brought with me from Finland. It was a Christmas present from Mr. Kelemen, a Hungarian refugee who sublet our kitchen for a little while during the winter war. The Germans had taken over his home country and luckily, he had escaped unscathed. The German-made erector set was truly a magnificent piece of work. It consisted of red and white metal plates, rails, pulleys, wheels and gears, little cranks and fasteners of all shapes and sizes, and even tiny wrenches and screwdrivers. It was the most fascinating present, truly a little boy's dream come true. The kit came with an illustrated instruction booklet showing how to build many wonderful things. I never tired of building contraptions like windmills, cranes, and steam engines. The diverse farm machinery gave me new ideas to create my own designs not pictured in the instruction booklet. One day I built a windmill, whose blades could rotate rapidly by turning a little crank. I was playing with the windmill outside, and as the blades turned faster and faster, one of them suddenly came loose and flew into the air. I looked for the missing part for a long time but could not find it. It was an indispensable part because it could be used for building other machines. I thought of Mr. Andersson, and I brought a similar part to the blacksmith shop. He examined it intently and then promised that he'd build me a replacement part. The new part fit perfectly with my erector set, although it wasn't painted like the original. But no matter, it made me very happy. I had acquired an interest in all things mechanical, which most likely influenced me to become a mechanical engineer in adulthood. Mr. Andersson was one of my best adult friends in Sweden.

I spent days roaming around the farm with its many large buildings, most of which were painted bright red with white trim. They were laid out in an L-shape with the main barn housing the horses and cows and the supply buildings on the other side. The supply buildings contained carriages, flat beds, saddles, and other tack. The sleighs, used in the wintertime, were stored here as well. It was fun to roam around there with its unique smell of axle grease, leather, and old hay. Sunlight seeped through cracks in the walls exposing a fine mist of dust which danced in the air. The most curious smell of all was the strong stench of rotten fish which came from barrels and barrels stored behind the shed. No one paid any attention to these forgotten herring-filled barrels, and I doubted that they ever would. For three years I remember smelling that pungent odor.

One day we had a terrible accident on the farm. The main barn building contained a cavernous loft used to store hay for the winter. To gain entry to the loft, a long ramp had been built with a wooden bridge spanning the end of the ramp through the large doors leading into the loft. Day after day, teams of horse-drawn carts brought the hay into the loft where it was sucked through large pipes hooked up to a suction pump and then blown into stacks reaching up to the ceiling. Trap doors located in the floor made it possible to feed the hay directly to the horses and cows.

Tragedy struck this day while two heavy draft horses pulled a hay-filled wagon up the ramp. As the farmer walked his team of horses up the steep slope, the wooden bridge suddenly gave way. Without warning, the horses crashed through the weakened bridge structure. The sound of breaking timber was muted by the horrifying squeals of the terrified animals. Landing on their backs on the hard ground below, the loaded hay wagon fell on top of them. They lay there, mortally wounded. The sight of their broken legs and bleeding injuries was more than I could bear. Farmhands came running from the barn in the hopes of helping the injured animals, but nothing could be done for them. Sven quickly retrieved a gun and mercifully shot them to put them out of their misery. The accident cast a pall over the farm. The agronomer was summoned, and he quickly came over to survey his loss. He was extremely upset about having lost two of his draft horses, not to mention the damage to the bridge. Placing no blame on anyone, he ordered the reconstruction of all the ramps as quickly as possible. It was getting late in the season, and it was imperative to fill the lofts to capacity before the bad weather set in. The screams of the dying horses kept me awake for many nights to come.

With the field work completed, I continued working odd jobs around the farm. I helped by opening the gates leading to the corrals and keeping the creaking hinges lubricated. One day I was opening one of the gates when it slipped out of my hands and landed on my big toe. I felt searing pain.

A farm hand, hearing my cry, came running and lifted the heavy gate, freeing my foot from the mud. With my big toe bleeding, I scampered home, where Aunt Sigrid tended to it quickly by cleaning off the mud and blood. She put a bandage on my foot and sent me back to work. My toenail fell off shortly after but a new one grew into its place.

The college students returned to their summer jobs. They filled in during the peak work periods, toiling in the fields, cleaning the barns, rewiring fences, and taking the horses to pasture. One late afternoon, while riding the horses to graze, a spooked horse reared unexpectedly, spilling the barebacked student rider. Unfortunately, he struck his head on the horse's hoof and fell to the ground, unconscious. His head wound bled profusely. A rapidly summoned neighbor woman tended to his injury to the best of her ability, but immediate medical care was required to treat his grave injury. The agronomer was called immediately to transport the student to the nearest physician in Målilla. His car was stored in one of the supply buildings, but unfortunately, the battery was dead. Sven, always ready to help, hitched a horse to the car and with the agronomer behind the wheel, managed to get the little car started. The injured student was lifted into the car. Blood had seeped through the heavy bandages around his head, soiling the upholstery. The agronomer, upon seeing the bloodied seat, swore out loud in disgust, temporarily forgetting the plight of the injured student. Regaining his composure, he departed for Målilla accompanied by the students' counselor.

Fortunately, the student recovered from his head injury enough to return to his home, but he was unable to continue his summer job on the farm. When he was well enough to travel, he paid us a short visit. His voice was slurred, and the accident prevented him from continuing his school studies the following semester.

The Butcher

The slaughterhouse was used on occasion to put down a horse gone lame or an old, unproductive cow. Mr. Bjork, the village butcher, would bring animals to shoot and then hoist the carcasses by the hind legs from the ceiling. The shed had no doors, so we kids had front row seats for these events. The butcher usually didn't mind us watching, provided we stayed out of his way. He was a gruff man with foul-smelling overalls and a long unkempt beard. He never seemed even remotely happy, probably due to the nature of his job. He first gutted and bled the animals, a large metal tub placed underneath to catch the draining blood, the entrails, and other rejected body parts. The smell was overpowering. After removing the heart and liver, which were the choice parts of the animal, he moved the now-cleaned carcass to the chilling room for aging. He shot a fox one day to keep it from killing the chickens, and since he had no business use for wild animals, he skinned it for the pelt and discarded the rest. It was a gruesome sight and I've never forgotten what that fox looked like without its fur coat. Its bulging eyes made it even more grotesque. The fox carcass ended up behind the pigsty by the cesspool, where rats would finish it off over the next few days. The pelt was draped over an anthill where millions of ants cleaned it up. Once clean, it could be tanned, and its fur used to line the insides of winter gloves.

Besides slaughtering farmyard animals, Mr. Bjork was also the pigsty keeper. His home sat on the far side of the outhouse on a slight knoll. His wife, a robust mother of two daughters who were both younger than me, was a sloppy housekeeper. In fact, the entire family seemed to care little about hygiene as their home was messy and dirty most of the time. Mr. Bjork always seemed angry, and due to the nature of his job, he smelled quite bad. The pigsty was located kitty-corner from the creamery, and hundreds of pigs wallowed in their muddy pens. Pigs can be very clean animals with the helping hand of a human. However, left to their own devices they will soon be covered with mud and feces. Overgrown rats patrolled the narrow walkways between the stalls, sometimes blindly running into one's legs. From time to time, I walked into this semi-dark dungeon out of curiosity more than desire, though it wasn't my favorite place to visit. But it provided a wonderful opportunity for me to bring my friends and observe the shocked looks on their faces upon seeing the large rats scurrying around.

Mr. Bjork was rather insensitive towards the pigs. He was seldom seen in the village, except when picking up his pay. No one wanted to stand near him, nor did anyone bother talking with him. But he supplied the village with all the pork products including chops, fresh ham, pigs' feet, spareribs, and ground pork for sausages and casings. He tried his best to keep the pens clean, but it was an overwhelming job at best. No one wanted to work there under those sordid conditions. The cesspool which was located directly behind the pigsty was overused since we lacked sewers or septic tanks, and the foul-smelling lake of wastewater extended into the woods with its brown, brackish water. It was fed by the wastewater from our house and the creamery, as well as the excrement from the pigsty. Not a pretty sight. No one ever seemed to get sick from living so close to it, but the long-term health effects were unknown. Our well water was never checked for bacteria. I suppose sometimes ignorance is bliss.

Mr. Bjork didn't take it kindly when I brought my friends to the pigsty, and he usually drove us out of there while cussing under his breath. Gigantic sows lying in their straw-filled pens cared for their piglets. The pregnant sows easily weighed over three hundred pounds. At times, a dozen of them were lined up, sucking on their mother. Occasionally a piglet was smashed to death by a careless sow, while some others succumbed to the hungry rats.

I watched Mr. Bjork castrate the piglets. He brought them outside into the sunlight where, sitting on a stump, he placed them on top of his leather apron. He doused their genitals with alcohol then slit their sacks open with a sharpened knife and expertly popped out their testicles and tossed them into a bucket. Ignoring the squeals of these little tykes, he went about his job in a professional manner. The castrated piglets ran off into the barnyard, seemingly unconcerned over this dastardly procedure.

One day Mr. Bjork had to slaughter an enormous sow, and I happened to be outside when I heard earsplitting squeals coming from the side of our house. I ran over to find the cause of the commotion. There was Mr. Bjork with another farmhand readying the sow for the kill. The village blacksmith had fashioned a special tool for anesthetizing large, hard-to-handle pigs. This strange looking implement consisted of an iron bar about three feet in length with a loop on one end. A long spike, sharpened on one end, was placed through the loop. The farmhand held this murderous-looking tool directly over the forehead of the unsuspecting animal and Mr. Bjork swung a large wooden mallet, quickly driving the spike into the sow's brain. The sow, never knowing what hit her, stumbled and fell over sideways, still breathing but oblivious to everything. While she lay there, Mr. Bjork cut her throat from one side to the other. The crimson blood gushed out from the jugular artery in spurts and was collected into a large, enameled dish. By the time the dish was full, the pig had taken her last breath. The entire process took but a few minutes.

Mrs. Bjork, standing nearby, picked up the blood-filled dish and took it up to her house, whipping it along the way with a wire whisk. Mixing flour and eggs with the fresh warm blood, she made pancakes that were "to die for." These were delicacies only available during times like these, and she always shared them with us. I liked eating them rolled up and doused with sugar. So tasty!

Mr. Bjork and his helper dragged the sow to the slaughterhouse where the carcass was hoisted up by its hind legs, ready to be butchered. The stomach was opened to expose the internal organs. Mr. Bjork gutted it quickly, discarding the bowels and the lungs. He was very careful not to puncture the bladder. The heart, liver, and kidneys were removed and tossed into a large bucket. He scraped the pig's hide carefully while we watched the process. Quickly, he cut off the pig's tail and threw it at us, grinning and exposing his tobacco-stained teeth. The carcass emitted a strange, unpleasant odor as it hung there in the summer breeze. Watching the proceedings was interesting in a ghoulish sort of way. The butcher cut off the pig's head to be used for making head cheese. Its feet were cleaned and pickled. The carcass was left to age for a few days. Lacking refrigeration, it was quartered, some of it smoked, and the rest packed in coarse salt. None of it was ever wasted. Mr. Bjork had also butchered the two horses lost in the hayloft incident. Horse meat, which is very lean, was considered a delicacy and only eaten under special circumstances.

Flowers and Pinecones

On her days off from the dairy, Aunt Sigrid took me for walks through the woods and meadows. She was eager to show me the very first spring flower, the blåsippa. We picked these delicate, blue flowers carefully and put them into tiny vases to decorate the kitchen table. Other flowers appeared later in the spring, but the blåsippa had special significance, signaling the beginning of spring. I began to pick assorted flowers and put up a small stand by the creamery loading dock. Farmers, after unloading their milk cans, often bought a few bouquets. This seasonal job filled my pockets with jingling change. Once again, I turned my earnings over to Uncle Pelle for safekeeping. Tutte seemed a little perturbed with my ventures. He thought that I was just a privileged kid from Finland and accused me of getting favors that he didn't have. At times I felt sorry for him. I was, after all, very lucky to be living with the Perssons.

Our school once proposed a pinecone-collection contest, and a prize was to be awarded to the school kid with the most cone-filled sacks. The burlap sacks were provided by the school and the contest was limited to children only. Despite the rules, Aunt Sigrid wanted to help me win the prize by picking pinecones with me. We went out in the evenings with baskets since the burlap sacks were too cumbersome to lug around. Dumping the pinecones into the sacks back at the dairy, we filled several of them in a short time. It was a time-consuming effort and each trip into the woods took us further away from the house. When the contest ended, we brought our four filled sacks to the schoolhouse by horse and buggy. I didn't get first prize but clinched the second, winning a book about a young lad traveling throughout Sweden. One of the competing kids claimed that he had seen Aunt Sigrid helping me pick pinecones, but he must have been mistaken because, when confronted with the accusation, Aunt Sigrid insisted that we had been mushroom picking. Some of the kids were upset and carried a grudge toward me. Thinking back, I can't believe that she had so wanted me to win the first prize that she had taken a chance to help me succeed.

Making Mischief

One day during the summer my foster parents were called out of town. Friends of the Perssons took over the basic operation of the creamery. Aunt Sigrid arranged for Ingrid, the older of two sisters living in the village, to look after me during their absence. Ingrid prepared our meals, and she kept the house tidy. I only saw her early in the morning and after returning home from school when I exchanged my school clothes for swimming trunks. Ingrid liked playing games, her favorite being hide and seek. There weren't many places to hide in the house and I easily found her in her hiding place behind the door. It was then my turn to hide, and while Ingrid counted to twenty with her eyes closed, I hid in the reservoir room. I wasn't supposed to go in there, as there was an eight-foot deep, open storage tank covering the entire room surrounded by a narrow walkway. The top of the tank was about four feet above the floor. The reservoir provided water for the creamery cooling tanks and for hosing down the floor. Entry to the reservoir room was limited to the inspection and maintenance of the pumps which brought water from the outside well.

Once I hid behind the tank, Ingrid began her search for me. She looked everywhere but couldn't find me. She never ventured inside my dark hiding place. The Perssons had cautioned her about the reservoir and instructed her to keep an eye on me lest I go there. Not being able to find me anywhere, she grew frightened that I might have gone in there and drowned. I could hear her footsteps scurrying through the house and her voice calling my name. Finally, she opened the door to the water reservoir and very cautiously stepped inside, expecting to find the worst. I jumped up suddenly, scaring her out of her wits. She cried out in fright, but upon hearing my laughter she regained her composure and began yelling at me. She was hopping mad by then. Though that was the last of our hide and seek games, each day I tried to think of new ways to trick her, and though I wasn't very nice to her, she took it all in stride. When Uncle Pelle and Aunt Sigrid returned at the end of the week, I feared the worst from Ingrid and was relieved to hear her say how much she had enjoyed looking after me.

Tutte and I played together every now and then when he wasn't mad at me for some reason or another. One day we walked along the railroad tracks, which was quite safe as the trains were infrequent. We could hear an approaching train in the distance and thus had plenty of time to jump to safety as the speeding train whooshed by. That day we were looking for wild strawberries along the tracks. Lacking a basket, we threaded the sweet berries on long stalks of grass, sometimes gathering ten or more to bring home for dessert. They were the sweetest berries one could find. The gravel road didn't bother our calloused feet as we jumped between the steel rails and over piles of rocks.

I spotted a snake coiled up on a large rock. It scared the daylights out of me, and I yelled out a warning to Tutte as he dashed behind me, for we had learned in school that this was a poisonous snake. The zigzag pattern adorning its back made it easy to recognize. Its bite, though not deadly, could make one ill. Being far away from a doctor gave us that much more reason to stay away from it. Laying my strands of strawberries on the ground, I found some rocks nearby. We decided to kill the snake on the spot. Luckily the first few rocks caused a lot of damage. With its head partly crushed, the snake rolled into a ball as it fell off the rock into a crevice. Hopefully it wouldn't be bothering us anymore. We resumed our berry-picking before returning home.

The next day we walked to our favorite swimming hole with other kids from the village. It was located across from the railroad station and the damaged power plant. A little inlet along the river made for a perfect place to swim. It was calm and safe, set away from the swift current. Since I still didn't know how to swim, I stayed in waist-deep water which was wonderfully cooling on a hot day. The older boys dove off protruding rocks and swam among the lily pads. We played there for a while and feeling refreshed from our dip, we headed for home along the dusty highway. On our homeward journey we passed an old, dilapidated barn which of course we had to explore in the hopes of finding treasure. Suddenly a terrible smell engulfed the air. To our surprise, we found a dead cow lying behind the barn, its belly swollen and crawling with flies. We found a long stick and tried to poke it into the bloated belly. Proving unsuccessful, we next threw rocks, but they just bounced off the dead carcass with a sickening sound. Luckily, we found an old rusty pitchfork inside the forgotten barn. Using our new tool, we pricked the extended belly which made a popping, hissing sound. Without warning, we were sprayed by a dark yellow liquid which shot out from the pierced belly. I had never smelled something so revolting in my life; it was simply horrible and reeked mercilessly as it squirted out in every direction. Dropping the pitchfork we ran to safety, lucky that we hadn't been thoroughly spattered.

Relating this story to Sven, he laughed and called us all sissies. Uncle Pelle was speechless and couldn't get over how we always managed to get ourselves into such fixes. He always told us how girls avoided such incidents, but I think that being a boy was more fun. Without uttering a word, Aunt Sigrid just shook her head sadly in disbelief.

George with Sigrid and Pelle.

Living the Life

Our summer weather in Ryningsnäs was usually warm and comfortable. At times one could predict an approaching thunderstorm by the smell in the air. The village roads, made of dirt, were narrow and subject to severe rutting when traveled upon by horse and buggy. Most wagons were fitted with steel-rimmed wooden wheels, though a few of the newer flatbed wagons sported rubber wheels that were far less destructive to the road surface. The ruts became deeper during prolonged rainfall and filled with water, which made it difficult for horses and wagons to navigate. It would have been cumbersome to drive an automobile on such a road. When the weather cleared the ruts eventually disappeared. As it was, the village had but one automobile which belonged to the agronomer, though he seldom drove it, preferring to get about on horseback. Consequently, his car was seldom used and usually sat in a shed near the barn. Most of the time the car's battery ran down which made it impossible to self-start. When he occasionally wanted to travel a farther distance, he would take his car and would

145

have to summon a ranch hand to help him get it started. Sven, having helped many times before, hitched one of the horses to the car and pulled it out from the shed and down the dirt road. The agronomer was able to kickstart it and drive away unfettered. We found it amusing to watch this spectacle, though we were careful not to reveal our true feelings to the "king of the village," as we called him in endearing terms. Such little events spiced up our otherwise mundane lives.

One day my foster parents were invited to go on a car trip. Uncle Pelle's wealthy cousin came to Ryningsnäs for a short visit in his own car, which of course created quite a stir. So here we were, suddenly whisked away in this large black sedan with four doors and extra jump seats directly behind the front seat. The wonderful smell of gasoline lingered in my nostrils as we left the dairy, conjuring the remembrance of adventure and travel. The Perssons had arranged for people to operate the creamery during their absence, and I got to leave school early, making sure not to miss out on this magnificent trip.

As we left our village my friends watched us with longing eyes. Being able to ride in a car was a special treat for us, by far more fun than riding in a horse-drawn cart. The big car turned slowly onto the main gravel highway, and we were on our way. Our driver headed southeast toward Oskarshamn, a beautiful seaport on the eastern coast of Småland. On our visit, we saw the world's longest bench. It was set in a hillside park that stretched from one end of the harbor to the other, filled with flowers and beautiful shrubs. We watched adults and children playing in the park, everyone dressed in their nice, well-pressed clothes and shiny shoes. On this clear sunny day, we could see the Gulf of Bothnia stretch out as far as the eye could see. Uncle Pelle told me that by sailing due east one would arrive in Latvia, one of the three Baltic states. From our lofty vantage point, we were able to watch five cargo ships, moored by the dock side, being loaded and unloaded by busy stevedores. I was fascinated watching the large cranes lift heavy pallets of assorted goods and lower their loads into cavernous cargo bays.

Our journey took us to a tiny restaurant where we feasted on Swedish meatballs and mashed potatoes. The food tasted even better when eating out, and in fact, this was my first experience dining in a restaurant, which made this a very special occasion. For dessert we enjoyed cream puffs with strong coffee. I never tired of eating these mouth-watering pastries.

Later in the afternoon we visited my foster parents' friends near the outskirts of Oskarshamn. Custom dictates that a smorgasbord be served to visiting guests and, sure enough, the table was soon filled with delicacies of all kinds, never mind that we were still full following our earlier dinner. There were sliced luncheon meats, thinly sliced horse meat, cold meatballs, several kinds of cheeses, wonderful breads, and more hot coffee. Unable to say no to our hosts, we filled our tummies again to the bursting point.

We spent the night in a separate guest cottage on comfortable beds with soft, down-filled blankets. It was quite an improvement over my straw-filled wooden bed. After enjoying a hearty brunch, it was time to return home, and I couldn't wait to ride in the big car again. I got to ride in the front seat for part of the return trip and boy, was that exciting. I would always remember this trip as it proved to be one of the great highlights while living in Sweden. Upon returning home, my friends greeted me with lots of questions. They considered me a very lucky boy to have had the opportunity to ride in an automobile (even bigger than the agronomer's) and to travel to the city of Oskarshamn.

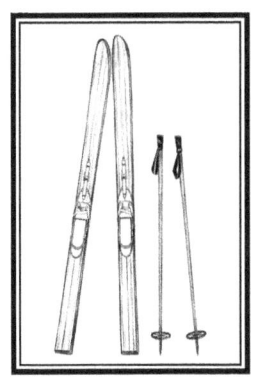

Through the Seasons

The summer turned to fall and then to winter. Snow whitened the landscape, transforming the fields into a winter wonderland. We enjoyed many sunny days when the snow glistened and beckoned us outside to play and breathe in the crisp, clean air. Uncle Pelle brought out a pair of skis which had belonged to their daughter, and which fit me well. The pasture in front of our house was a perfect place for cross-country skiing as most of the land was flat with a few hilly areas here and there, and it wasn't long before my ski trails crisscrossed the pasture in every direction.

Our school held a cross-country skiing race for the students, and I entered with most of my school chums. The course meandered through the woods, across ditches, over fences, down some slopes, and up a few steep hills. It proved a lot harder than it first appeared. I finished fourth in my class out of eight, which was certainly not the best, but I was nevertheless proud of my accomplishment. We received ribbons for having competed in this winter event which was enjoyed by all.

149

When the weather warmed a little, the wet snow provided opportunities to build snow forts and have snowball fights. The moonlit landscape was especially beautiful on cold crisp nights. On cold winter walks the snow crackled and sparkled under our feet.

On one relatively warm winter day I went for a hike with Tutte and his older brother on a hillside overlooking the winding farm road below. Unfortunately, this was going to be one of those embarrassing days which would be hard to live down. We decided to undress and run around in the snow wearing only our birthday suits, which seemed exciting at the time. We had run to the edge of the hillside when we heard raucous laughter coming from behind us. It turned out to be Per and his brother Gunnar, the schoolteacher's sons. They had been spying on us for some time, following from a safe distance, and when they suddenly appeared from behind some bushes, they burst out laughing, pointing at us accusingly. At first, we were startled but soon felt totally destroyed with shame and fear of the aftermath. We knew that they would not keep this a secret and, after all, why should they? We soon became the laughingstock of the village. How long would it take to live this one down? My foster parents didn't know what to make of it, but they did save me from embarrassment by not talking about it.

The holiday season was soon upon us. Aunt Sigrid had given me a wall calendar for the month of December which had thirty-one little closed doors superimposed over a Christmas theme. Each day I opened one little door from which appeared a scene from the Holy Bible. There were shepherds and their sheep, the wise men traveling in the desert, the pyramids of Egypt, and one door opened to depict a Christmas ham. I looked forward to each day when I could open another door. It was no fair peeking ahead since once the door was opened it couldn't be closed again without telltale marks. The month of December just crept by, oh so slowly. It seemed the approaching Christmas Eve would never come.

Santa Lucia Day is a special day in Sweden and is celebrated on December 13. In large families, the oldest daughter would dress in a long white gown and wear a wreath of freshly cut evergreen branches with white candles tied securely to the wreath. The lights would then be dimmed and the candles lit. Santa Lucia would bring her parents a tray with steaming cups of coffee and sweet rolls. Everyone in the procession would sing the Santa Lucia song, making this a most festive occasion. This custom was followed throughout Sweden, and I witnessed it at the Morstams' home.

We felled our Christmas tree in the nearby forest and brought it into the house on Christmas Eve. We decorated it with real candles attached to the sturdy branches along with homemade trinkets, ornaments, and hard candy. I had never seen a Christmas tree in Finland, so this was a special occasion for me. Uncle Pelle opened a box of Golden Delicious apples which he had saved for these festive days. The apples had been stored for several weeks and were each wrapped in white tissue paper. They were delicious and we ate them with gusto. I had no clue as to how he had acquired these wonder fruits.

Christmas Eve finally arrived, and Uncle Pelle dressed up as Santa Claus, and I never suspected that it was him in the Santa suit. Oh, to be young and innocent. Santa brought me a deck of Old Maid playing cards, an ink pen with a bottle of ink, a pad of writing paper, and a pair of winter boots. My gift to Uncle Pelle and Aunt Sigrid was a heart made from red and green paper which I made at school. It wasn't much but they cherished it just the same.

We ate quietly by candlelight. Aunt Sigrid prepared a small pork roast and boiled potatoes. In the absence of a radio, we sang Christmas carols and told stories about the past. Though it was frigid outside, our house was warm from the heat provided by the kitchen stove which gave off enough heat for our two rooms. It never crossed my mind as to how small our home really was; it always seemed large to me.

When summer finally arrived again, it was time to make a trip to Kalmar, a beautiful old city on the Gulf of Bothnia. We traveled to Kalmar by electric train, which was quiet, non-polluting, and fast, making the trip fly by. Since Ryningsnäs was not served by one of these speedy trains we had to take the local steam-powered train to a nearby city and then transfer onto the Kalmar train. Business offices, stores, and quaint little shops lined the waterfront streets. Kalmar was known for its castle, built during the early days of the Swedish kingdom to protect the city from pirates and enemies. The turreted castle is a magnificent work of art and remains a tourist attraction to this day. People come from far and wide to view this massive landmark, which evokes scenes of battle between knights in shining armor mounted on powerful white steeds.

Our destination in Kalmar was a visit to Optiker Tottie, an optician, who would be examining my eyes and who would fit me with a new pair of glasses with an updated prescription. I had the misfortune of needing glasses since the age of four, and I hated wearing them as my friends called me "four-eyes" or "the professor." The glasses would fog up unmercifully when entering a warm house from the snowy outdoors. When bumped, they would move out of adjustment and be uncomfortable, and the dusty fields coated the lenses with a layer of dirt causing them to smear. However, they did help me see better and I eventually got used to wearing them daily.

Optiker Tottie was tall, which is not unusual for Swedish men. He was witty and full of practical jokes, which made the exam seem like fun. I read the eye charts with each eye, and he fitted me with round, black-rimmed glasses which I didn't at all like, but which I got used to in time. While waiting for my glasses to be ready we walked around the city and window-shopped for hours. We stopped at a little café by the harbor and treated ourselves to a smorgasbord. Little sandwiches adorned the counters, and we picked several tasty-looking treats. Our train took us back home and I wouldn't return to Kalmar until 1972 accompanied by my wife and daughters.

Returning Home to Finland

The Voyage Home

Sylvi, Bertta and George.

After three years, the heavy fighting in Finland finally subsided and the Finnish government announced that it would be safe for children to return to their homes. Uncle Pelle and Aunt Sigrid prepared me for my return trip. When visiting Kalmar, they had purchased a new suit with knickerbocker pant legs, fashionable new shoes and socks, shirts, underwear, and accessories. My earnings from working on the farm, which Uncle Pelle had saved for me, paid for all my clothing. My foster parents would have been unable to make the purchase, being a poor working-class couple. They were very proud of my accomplishments.

All my friends were invited to the Perssons' home for my farewell party. I was truly saddened to have to leave everyone behind, but that was not the least of my worries because I had completely forgotten how to speak Finnish and I was more than a little frightened about how I would cope in the Finnish schools. I would be entering the fourth grade, and it would really be a challenge. And how would my mother feel when I couldn't greet her in my native tongue? I would be in new surroundings again as my mother had moved to a different part of the city. Much like my arrival in Sweden, I had no idea what was now ahead of me.

I had mixed feelings about having to leave Ryningsnäs and my dear foster parents. Uncle Pelle had been like a father to me, a fatherless child. No more fresh dairy products like a slice of wonderful cheese, a small cupful of rich cream, a dollop of yogurt. I had learned to love life on the farm, to be around farm animals, to pester Sven and to play with all my friends. It was going to be so different to live in a big city, relearn the Finnish language, attend a large public school, and make new friends. I felt uprooted, torn away from my wonderful foster mom and dad. What a quandary.

On the other hand, I yearned for the excitement of travel and of seeing my mother and new home. The remaining days went by too quickly, and I suddenly found myself back at the Ryningsnäs railroad station, standing between Uncle Pelle and Aunt Sigrid, waiting for my train to arrive. I could tell that, despite the smiles on their faces, they were really crying on the inside. They had grown tremendously fond of me despite the embarrassing moments, our petty quarrels, and even the burnt forest. They cherished the happy moments, the Sunday walks, my helping hand with the firewood and drinking water, and my practical jokes.

Once again, I was labeled like a suitcase: decorated with

a necklace which had destination tags, transfer slips, and my personal identification with my final destination clearly checked and re-checked. The conductor on the train would guarantee a safe arrival at my next stop.

We saw the train in the distance with its stack spewing steam and smoke, and we heard the chugging of the locomotive approaching the station house, then its screeching halt. It was time to say our final goodbyes. Climbing up the steps into the waiting coach, and pausing on the platform, I saw Uncle Pelle and Aunt Sigrid waving their hands, trying to hide their tears. They gave me encouraging smiles as they waved. I was a big boy now, nine and a half years old – old enough to be traveling by myself.

With a mighty jerk the train lurched forward, slowly at first with each chug of the locomotive, then with increasing speed. Uncle Pelle and Aunt Sigrid ran next to my car until the end of the station platform, waving frantically and blowing kisses in my direction. But soon, they were out of sight. The train headed for Nässjö where I was to change onto an electric train headed for Stockholm. My sadness was beginning to diminish with each kilometer as the excitement of travel replaced the anguish of my departure.

My next train was right on time and a courteous railroad official escorted me to my new assigned seat. Soon we were whizzing northeast to Stockholm. The lush countryside quickly unfolded with the sound of clicking made by the steel wheels rolling on the smooth steel tracks.

Arriving at the grand station in Stockholm, the capital of Sweden, we found the city bathed in bright sunlight. Again, a polite escort brought me to a large room within the railroad station which was filled with other boys and girls destined to return to their respective homes. No longer alone, I studied the others with guarded suspicion, but soon broke out with hundreds of questions: "Where did you live?" "Did you like your foster parents?" "Are you glad to return home to Finland?" "Where do your parents live?" Their responses ranged in emotions, from having loved living in Sweden to hating it with a vengeance, and to being extremely relieved to return home as well as dreading the return. My feelings were mirrored with some of the replies, and I felt so sad for the children who had not enjoyed their stay. Some Finnish kids were to remain in Sweden permanently because their parents had been killed during the war. Others wanted to stay there because their home lives were anything but pleasant. Goran, my close Finnish friend, wanted to stay in Sweden indefinitely. All these various situations would have to be settled legally.

Our chaperones brought us dockside and we boarded the SS *Brynhild*, the vessel which had brought me across the Gulf of Bothnia three years ago during the bitter winter of 1941. Our cabins had four bunks which we fought over with cries of delight and some desperation. Our unruly behavior and constant running around in the passageways proved taxing to the ship's crew. The dinner bell sounded and restored some semblance of calm. These delicious meals filled our hungry tummies, and I wondered what I would be eating when I finally arrived home.

The anchors were raised, and the ship inched away from the dock, slowly at first, then picking up speed as it coursed by the myriad of islands surrounding the city of Stockholm. The open sea lay ahead on our fifteen-hour journey. Summer sailing was a complete contrast to the tortuous winter. The icebreaker ships were docked, awaiting their use during the cold winter months.

We were ushered to our respective cabins, and a single porthole allowed us to peer outside. Daylight lingered until eleven o'clock and, finding it impossible to fall asleep, I tossed and turned in my bunk, thinking about my arrival in Finland and meeting my mother after a three-year absence.

We found our morning breakfast tasty and delightful. The sea was calm, and we observed other ships sailing by, sliding through the glassy water. We spent a lot of time outside, walking the decks. The wind picked up and our eyes watered to the point where we could barely keep them open.

My thoughts returned to my three adventurous years in Sweden. I thought of my foster parents and of my little farm home in Ryningsnäs. Memory turned to the agronomer, and I realized that he had selected a perfect group of people to serve our village. Each member had a special place with their individual talents, enabling the community to function smoothly. I was going to miss my friends whom I had met at school. My teachers, Ms. Edstrom and Mr. Morstam, made such a positive impact on my young life. I had learned to read, write, and speak the Swedish language. Sweden had offered so much help to war-torn Finland. My years there had turned out to be a wonderful learning experience which helped to shape my future life.

The children's excitement reached its peak as the SS *Brynhild* slowly sailed into the south harbor of Helsinki. The day was magnificent, with the bright blue of the sky overhead. The skyline of the city sparkled like a diamond. The Great Church of Finland was visible with its green, star-studded dome; the Russian Orthodox church, dubbed the "onion church," stood there majestically; the President's Palace and the open-air farmer's market came into view with hundreds of shoppers lined up around the counters. As the ship neared port, we could see the welcoming committee of mothers and fathers anxiously waiting to catch a glimpse of their sons and daughters. I was standing by the railing, looking at the people gathered below and hoping to spot my mother in the crowded throng.

We docked at last, and the final hawser was secured. I scanned the crowd for a familiar face. I spotted my mother waving a little Finnish flag and smiling from ear to ear. The gangplank was secured to the deck railing and the gates opened, allowing children to disembark the ship. I waited my turn to walk down the gangway to my teary-eyed mother. She greeted me with a hug and spoke hurriedly in Finnish. I couldn't understand the words very well. She introduced me to her companion, Kalle. He was bilingual in Swedish and Finnish, so I spoke to him, and he translated for my mother. She seemed a little disappointed that I couldn't respond in Finnish. Kalle's Swedish accent was totally different from the sing-song dialect spoken in Småland, but it was understandable. My luggage finally arrived and Kalle carried my suitcase with ease.

It was 1944 and the fighting between the Russians and the Finns had ceased with the Russians suing for peace. Little did I know that the economic situation had continued to be less than perfect. I would soon find out what life was really like in my native country. We headed toward the farmer's market, and I spotted a stand filled with bright red tomatoes. They looked so appetizing. However, Finland was in the midst of a severe inflationary period and only the well-heeled could afford to indulge. My mother looked at me sadly and explained that they were too expensive. She simply could not afford to buy even one of them. I was disappointed of course, but soon found out that I would have to adjust to a new lifestyle very quickly.

We left the marketplace and boarded a streetcar to the center of Helsinki where we transferred onto another streetcar and finally arrived near my new home. Mother had moved to a new part of town during my absence and now lived in Töölö, on the outskirts of the city. Our home was near a rather nice swimming beach. A majestic chapel provided access to a cemetery that had nicely manicured shrubs and bushes with meandering gravel walkways. There was absolutely no litter in sight. Polished headstones adorned each grave and thoughtfully placed flowers were everywhere. These pathways offered wonderful opportunities for Sunday walks.

Our building was four stories and we lived on the main floor. The entry was through a large, locked front door and we walked into the building along a hallway with highly polished floors. Mother opened our door, which was near the elevator, and we entered our apartment. It consisted of a small hallway, a washroom, a tiny kitchen, and a living room that had a small alcove for my bed, sheltered by a curtain extending from wall to wall. Mother's bed was in the living room and doubled as a sofa by day. Two easy chairs and a table furnished the room. She had purchased a large bookcase with sliding glass doors and a nice marble-topped table with a mirror encased by a gold-colored frame.

The kitchen was furnished with a large wooden table and two benches. Two heavy duty sewing machines, designed to handle heavy fur coats, sat side by side against one wall. A massive plywood sheet rested on top of the table and numerous pelts were nailed, fur side down, to its surface. They were being stretched and shaped so that they could be fashioned into a fur coat. The pelts were oriented such that the direction of the fur was the same. Mother used the special sewing machines to sew them together. Each pelt measured twenty-five by seven centimeters in size. Before putting on the lining, the fur coat consisted of as many as a hundred little pelts. Winter fur coats were quite popular in Finland, and my mother had further refined her skills during my stay in Sweden. She had become quite proficient in the business of making and selling fur coats to her customers. She had become an entrepreneur, working directly from her home. Her work hours varied greatly: during busy times she worked ten hours a day, sometimes seven days a week. Customers came directly to her with requests for new coats, repairs, and fittings, and she was paid in cash at the time of delivery.

There were many nights when I could hear her hammering pelts to be stretched. Besides working on the pelts, there was a lot of sewing by hand. Heavy felt materials were sewn on the inside of the coat for insulation from the bitter winter cold, followed by decorative lining. It was painstaking work. Many times, her thimbles wore thin, and she suffered injuries to her fingers when the heavy-duty needles required to penetrate the tough hides punctured the thimbles and her fingers. At times infection set in, making it excruciatingly difficult to work. It certainly was a hard way to make a living. I soon became accustomed to the tapping sound and eventually stopped paying attention to the noise. Her friend Kalle paid her a visit now and then, but Mom was too busy to date due to her impassioned will to work and remain independent.

Surprisingly, I regained my native language rather quickly which made it much easier to communicate with my mother and new friends. I met a boy called Timo whose building was kitty-corner from mine, and he became my closest friend. His father was the manager of their building. Timo and I played together almost every day on a nearby rock hill. Much of southern Finland, near the coast, was rocky and inhospitable. We termed our playground "the big rock." It was part of a large park with pathways and well-manicured lawns. Benches were placed along the pathways, and people took advantage of the park in the summertime. One could always find people enjoying "the big rock" for sunning, reading, or playing with their children. During the wintertime the rock provided great slopes for skiing and sledding.

Imagining America

Preparations

George with violin.

In 1947, my mother convinced herself once and for all to make the big move to America. She broke the news to me one day and it was the most exciting thing to ever happen to me and I couldn't sleep at night at the mere thought of it. Just imagine, having the chance to travel to America, the land with paved streets of gold, cowboys and Indians, luscious fruit dangling from the trees, movie stars, skyscrapers, multi-engine airplanes, and beautiful homes. Oh, I was ready to go right away.

Mother started the process of obtaining visas and passports for our impending trip. This was going to take a long time and a lot of money, much of it passing to greedy hands under the table. She sold our small condo and found ways to dispose of our furnishings. Since we could travel with only one suitcase and one travel trunk, I had to sell my meager possessions to my friends and anyone else who wanted my treasures. My Aunt Sylvi gave us a wooden trunk which had a curved lid and small compartments on the inside for loose items.

But what to do with our Finnish currency, as it was useless in the United States? Kalle, my mother's good friend, had an answer to this perplexing question. He promised to buy Swedish kronor, a hard currency accepted in the USA, and to find a way to transport this money overseas in a secretive way. This was necessary because the United States government only allowed a limited amount of currency to be brought into the country from abroad. Kalle had an idea how to bring the currency to America undetected. He took Aunt Sylvi's wooden trunk to a local furniture repair service and with the help of the proprietor, drilled a series of deep holes in the edges of the trunk. He then rolled the Swedish kronor and stuffed them into these holes. Wooden plugs were then tapped into the ends and painted black, and each edge was then reinforced with metal angle irons and painted with a glossy black finish. The trunk looked very natural indeed. The money would ultimately be removed by splintering the edges of the trunk. These unsightly broken edges could then be filled with a hard-setting putty and the trunk repainted with the attached angle irons. Once repaired, the trunk would serve as a beautiful piece of furniture for storing blankets and tablecloths.

I spent many days selling my personal things to my friends. Also in my possession was the large roll of 35mm film which I had brought back from Sweden and was a part of the movie projector package that Uncle Pelle and Aunt

Sigrid had given to me for Christmas. I sold the film by the meter to my buddies who valued it for its flammability. Any kid with a good spyglass could ignite it with ease on a bright sunny day, and spyglasses were still the rage. We weren't pyromaniacs, but we loved to build little fires around "the big rock." My spyglass had been returned to me just before leaving Sweden, as Uncle Pelle had safeguarded it after I started the forest fire in Ryningsnäs. I kept the money from my sales, now exchanged into Swedish kronor, and I wanted this hard-earned money close to me until my arrival in America.

Little by little Mother managed to sell our furnishings. She was saddened when her life's possessions disappeared piece by piece. I must admit that my mother had a lot of courage to make this big change in her life. It was risky to leave her homeland and to face an uncertain future in another country.

The day finally came for our shots. I didn't look forward to getting them because I was afraid of needles and the antiseptic smell of medicine at the clinic. Not only that, but my arm was to be sore for days from the multitude of shots. We were required to visit the American Consulate in Helsinki prior to our departure, where we found, to our great surprise and disappointment, that our Finnish passports and visas were invalid. Mother had spent a fortune on them, not to mention the bribes that had been extracted from her. She was told that she had to acquire an American passport because, unbeknownst to her, she had been born in Waukegan, Illinois in 1906 and was therefore an American citizen. Grandfather had emigrated to America in 1904 with his wife, but he never liked living there and decided to move back to Finland in 1908, after Mother was born. I never found out the reason why he chose to return.

It was quite easy and not terribly expensive to obtain American passports and luckily the delay was of no consequence since the trip was only a few days away. My grandfather and Aunt Maiju arrived in Helsinki a few days before our departure. They were melancholic and teary-eyed, knowing that we would be leaving them forever. My grandfather was getting old, as was Maiju. Aunt Sylvi had hopes that the trip would not work out and we would stay in Finland, but she knew better than to express them to us.

The last few days crawled by, and I couldn't wait. My best friend Timo was speechless. We had been friends ever since I returned from Sweden in 1944 and had done everything together: playing on "the big rock," skiing to Seurasaari Island over the ice in the wintertime, and reading books together during the long nights of winter.

Finally, the big day arrived. Mother and I were all decked out in our best. I remember that we got into two taxi cabs, accompanied by Kalle, Aunt Sylvi, Maiju, Grandfather, and Timo. We arrived at the Helsinki railroad station and boarded a train bound for Turku, Finland. I still look at the picture taken of us on the railway platform and realize that I was the only one smiling amid all those sad faces. It was a bittersweet farewell, but I was on cloud nine. The railroad conductor urged us to get into the coach because it was time to depart. We found our seats quickly and sat down with our noses glued to the window. As the train lurched forward and started to move, I could see Aunt Sylvi and Timo running along the station platform until they faded from view. Our big adventure had begun.

The Trip of a Lifetime

Helsinki Central Station –
George with Sylvi and Bertta (center).

Once our train bound for Turku departed the Helsinki station, mother cried quietly but I was too excited to think about tears. It was a beautiful day in early June as the clickety-clack of steel wheels against rails reminded us that we would not be coming back to Finland for a long time, if ever. The landscape unfolded magically outside our window, exposing flat farmland, spartan homes and barns, thousands of birch trees, and little lakes, of which Finland claims to have over 60,000. One could find an occasional Finnish flag waving in the distance, its colors depicting the blue sky as a cross set against white clouds. Now we were headed for the land flying the stars and stripes which added to the excitement.

We arrived in Turku, a seaport on the southwest corner of Finland, in four hours' time.

As we disembarked the train we were brought to the waterfront to board, once again for me, the Swedish ship SS *Brynhild*, which would sail to Stockholm across the Gulf of Bothnia. This was to be an overnight trip. We spent the first night in the port in Turku preparing to sail early the next morning. Our cabin was small but comfortable, the crew was polite, and the food was extraordinarily good. The dining room seated all the passengers with room to spare. The Swedes sure knew how to bake delicious bread. We feasted on Swedish meatballs, mashed potatoes and carrots, and a lingonberry pudding for dessert. While dining I met a boy my age, Risto, and after dinner, we scurried all over the decks of the SS *Brynhild*.

We were invited to the movies, where we watched an American musical dubbed in Swedish. I had a full command of Swedish and enjoyed the movie, and though my mother didn't speak Swedish or English, she enjoyed the singing. It was time to return to our little cabin for a night's rest, but I was too excited to sleep, tossing and turning most of the night. I must have dozed off, however, as the ship's engines woke me up in the early morning and we were soon underway.

I raced outside to the deck and watched the beautiful water rushing by. Hundreds of little islands dotted the gulf, forming an archipelago, some too small to be inhabited, others with red-painted houses with white trim around the windows. The ever-present birch trees partially hid the red buildings.

My new-found friend Risto and I had so much fun examining this wonderful ship. We walked from stem to stern, checking out every nook and cranny. The weather was perfect with a healthy breeze blowing. I kept thinking that I didn't want this trip to ever end. Gosh, no school to worry about, no homework, only fun, fun, fun. And to top it off, America ahead!

Mother and I went to the dining room and had the most delicious dinner. Once more the flavorful breads with rich butter, and the meatballs, oh how good they tasted with mashed potatoes and assorted vegetables. Finland was still recovering from the war years and ordinary groceries were prohibitively expensive. Mother cooked in a very spartan manner with her meager means.

Our cabin was tiny with two bunks and a porthole afforded us light by day and a black hole by night. It was meant just for sleeping and nothing more. We were lulled to sleep by the gentle swaying of the ship, and I could hear water coursing against the hull as it beckoned me to dreamland.

I woke up early in the morning as the SS *Brynhild* sailed into the harbor of Stockholm. Islands by the dozen glided slowly by and several smaller boats were anchored near the shores as we approached port. It didn't take long to dock. The tall city hall stood nearby, built of red brick and sporting three golden crowns from the steeple, and the Royal Palace was visible nearby. Shiny automobiles, colorful streetcars, and city buses coursed back and forth. The sidewalks were filled with well-dressed people walking to and fro. The sound of the city was captivating and young lads were waving at our vessel and yelling greetings to the passengers.

We prepared to disembark and congregated on the main deck above. Our luggage was brought to us, what little there was of it. Soon deckhands led us to the dock and brought our baggage along. We were ushered aboard a large bus which quickly took us to the main railroad station not far from the port. Having lived in Sweden for three years I remembered that the traffic moved forward in the left lanes, not on the right like in Finland. It still seemed so strange to me, and I wondered how the traffic moved in America. I could hardly wait to arrive in New York City.

We boarded an electric train destined for Göteborg, a western port south of the tip of Norway. The train trip was fascinating as the Swedish countryside raced by outside my window. All the buildings seemed so large and well-kept in comparison to Finland's austere countryside. These obvious differences were noticeable and illustrated the fact that Sweden had remained neutral during World War II. No evidence was visible of the scars of war, of bombed ruins, or of people hobbling along with crutches. How lucky they had been during the war years.

Boarding the Ship for New York City

7

We arrived in the busy city of Göteborg later that afternoon. Railroad stations were always so interesting to me. I was impressed by the electric locomotives with their pantographs reaching up to the electric wires above. We were once again transported by bus to the International Port of Göteborg. Our ship, the SS *Drottningholm*, one of three ships of the Swedish American lines, was docked here, waiting for us to embark on a ten-day cruise to New York City. It was the oldest and smallest of the three, the MS *Kungsholm* and the MS *Gripsholm* being the other two. Our ship was the largest I'd ever seen, and I couldn't wait to board.

[7] Public Domain, https://en.wikipedia.org/w/index.php?curid=64157193

Our cabin turned out to be very small and it was in the bowels of the ship. Undoubtedly it must have been the cheapest berth available. Two pairs of double bunks filled the cabin. Mother took the lower and I opted for the upper. Lillian, the third passenger, took the other lower bunk, leaving one unoccupied. The porthole was closed with a tight cover making it impossible to look outside. I suspect that we were probably underwater anyway, and I was disappointed with this arrangement.

Suddenly, there was a lot of noise outside our cabin. I begged mother to let me go outside to investigate the source, reminding her that I was twelve years old and growing up quickly. She finally gave me permission and I jumped out of the cabin into the hold which was bathed in daylight and smelled of raw ocean air. The deck had been opened revealing the gaping hold. I quickly realized what was going on. I could hear winches operating noisily, lowering cargo into the hold which was held together by large nets made of heavy ropes. Down and down the loaded nets went to men ready to unload them. They were yelling and at times, cursing loudly. A foul smell drifted from the dirty holds, and here we were in this undesirable setting for the next ten days. My heart sank, but not for long because we were to set sail within a few hours. It didn't take long before the hold was closed tightly, and the overhead hatch battened down. Gosh, it was dark with the daylight blocked out.

I climbed the stairway to the next deck which looked more like I'd pictured a ship in my imagination. Long passageways ran fore and aft with cabin doors situated on both sides of the aisle. I bet that these cabins were a lot nicer than ours. People shuffled up and down the aisle. The next deck revealed more cabins. Climbing a further deck, I encountered a large dining room with numerous round tables which busy waiters were setting for the evening meal. Ample daylight illuminated the dining room and the adjoining mess hall where chefs prepared the evening's dinner. Suddenly I regained my enthusiasm for the voyage, putting away my thoughts of our austere cabin. Mother would be pleased as well. I ran down the stairway to our cabin and excitedly told her of my findings. She broke out in a big grin and wanted to accompany me for a shipboard walk. I felt like a tour guide, being able to show her what I'd discovered.

At dinnertime we walked to the dining room and were shown our permanently assigned table for eight people. Lillian, our roommate, was already seated, as well as a family of three with a twelve-year-old boy and an older couple bound for Canada. When the waiters brought our dinner, Mother and I marveled at the bountiful servings, which by today's standards would have been quite ordinary. We met our table guests and had somewhat of a difficult time conversing with them due to language differences. My mother only spoke Finnish, making it difficult to carry on conversation. Lillian, who spoke Finnish as well, was also from Helsinki and heading to Toronto. The family of three was Swedish and their boy Gordon and I hit it off from the start. They were from Skåne, Sweden and were immigrating to America in search of a better life. The older couple was German and kept to themselves. They seemed displeased with having to share our table.

While we enjoyed our first meal, we suddenly realized that the SS *Drottningholm* was underway for the open waters. The sailing was smooth, which made our dinner very soothing. We went to the social hall after dinner and enjoyed the beautiful, dark wood interiors, decorated with paintings and comfortable furnishings. Large windows lined both sides of the hall to reveal the open ocean. Seagulls soared alongside the ship, occasionally diving down just over the waves.

Gordon and I went walking along the covered outdoor walkways and were refreshed by the sea air. We found our way to the bow where the fierce breeze made walking somewhat difficult. Gosh, this was so much fun. We saw other ships, cargo and passenger, on both sides. The sun was still shining brightly but it would soon disappear into the horizon. The long days of summer continued until eleven o'clock. After dusk we returned to our cabins.

It was rather difficult to fall asleep as my bunk was not very comfortable, but the smooth motion of the ship made sleeping bearable. The toilets were on the aft side of the covered hold and were quite large, with open showers and several stalls. They were, for the moment, clean, but would not remain so for long.

The next day was calm and smooth. Open seas greeted us, and at first, we were awed, but after a while they grew monotonous. I knocked on Gordon's cabin and soon we went to explore other sections of the ship. Lifeboats, covered with tarps, lined both sides of the gangplanks. I wondered if they were really of any use in stormy seas and hoped that we wouldn't have to find out. We tried to get up to the bridge to see the control room but were turned away by an unfriendly crew member.

One day we discovered that the deck boards were sealed with a very pliable tar-like substance. We found that we could dig up the tar and soon had gobs of it at hand. Gordon made a softball sized one and mine was a little smaller. After more digging, our tar balls got bigger and bigger. Now we could use them for playing soccer on the deck surface! But our game didn't last very long. A crew member caught us playing and soon realized where we had gotten the stuff. He cursed loudly and took us by the scruff of our necks, herding us into crew quarters for questioning. We understood what he was saying and why he was so darned angry. He threatened to throw us overboard, scaring us half to death. The tar-like substance was a watertight sealer between the deck boards and performed a very necessary function. As twelve-year-old boys, we had no idea that we had compromised the watertightness of the deck. He finally brought us to our parents and made several threats to prevent us from doing it again. My mother was very angry and I was grounded for the rest of the day.

Each evening after dinner they showed movies in the ship's theater, which seated about fifty people. We saw some American musicals and westerns in which the cowboys killed the "bad" Indians. I could hardly wait to get to America so that I could meet real cowboys. I was also looking forward to eating grapes right out of the trees. Americans were so lucky to be rich and to live such fun-filled lives.

The Storm

On the third day at sea the sky turned gray, and the wind was blowing so briskly that the swells moved the ship up and down. Gordon and I were running outside under the covered walkways getting sprayed with saltwater. The ship was starting to rock more intensely, and it became more and more difficult to keep one's balance. The horizon was no longer visible. There were only waves and each one seemed to grow taller and taller. I became a little nervous as I wondered how bad this storm would become and decided to make my way back inside.

I was waiting for the lunch bell to sound so I could quell my hunger. It seemed that I was always hungry and looking forward to the wonderful food. Finally, it was time for lunch, but my mother wasn't very hungry. She was frightened by the storm and was on the verge of becoming seasick. She ate very sparingly and left early to return to her berth. The gently rolling ship affected some people more than others.

As the day wore on, the swells seemed to increase in size and fury. The ship's steward made an announcement that all doors leading to the promenades would be locked, thus preventing passengers from getting drenched by the crashing waves and from possibly being swept overboard. This seemed rather surreal but also exciting since we had no idea what to expect. The doors were to be shut until the storm had subsided. As each hour passed, the swells became stronger. We had entered the North Sea which is notorious for rough sailing. The ship began to rock and roll with each passing wave, and we had to hang on to the railings and furnishings to remain standing. It took a long time to acquire sea legs, but with each passing wave it became a little easier to move about.

The skies grew darker, and the sea was broiling with mountains of waves visible in all directions. The ship lunged upward to the top of one wave and then suddenly dropped into the trough, leaving me temporarily weightless. My stomach turned upside-down as we rode the wave downward, and as the ship bottomed out, I felt twice as heavy as normal, as if someone had pushed me tightly against the floor. The ship moaned and groaned and threatened to split into two, but it miraculously held together. This was getting uglier by the minute. Would we even make it to America?

Dinner was postponed due to the rough seas. Dinnerware would not fare well on the tables, and what's more, passengers were becoming seasick in droves. Mother was bedridden with a bucket by her side, though Lillian fared much better. She was sitting in the bar clutching a drink in her hand. She looked a little green though, and I wasn't placing my bets on her health.

The ship moved up and down, creaking her way into the ocean depth and rising with great force to the crest of the next wave. But the worst was not over, not by a long shot. The entire night was one that I would like to forget. And early in the morning, the ship began to roll as well. My stomach didn't like this motion one bit. The rocking motion had become predictable, but the rolling added another dimension. This undulating motion was sure to sicken the most experienced seaman, so how could a landlubber like me endure it?

I felt my stomach lurching and had to make a run for the lavatory. This was a big mistake, as it was filled with passengers throwing up, not in the toilets but all over the slick floor. The stench was so overpowering that I couldn't remain in there. As I tried to hurry outside, I slipped and fell on the vomit-covered floor and nearly lost my dinner. I had to get out quickly and find fresh air lest I become sick also. I somehow maintained my balance and kept from throwing up, but my clothing reeked of vomit, and I had to clean up quickly. Our cabin wasn't far from the lavatory, thank goodness, and I managed to find clean clothing, change quickly, and climb upstairs to the social hall. Somehow, I managed to remain unaffected by the bucking motion of the ship. The rolling was nauseating, and I fought the feeling of motion sickness. To this day I have never been affected by the rolling sea. Gordon had succumbed to seasickness and so I was left to my own devices. Mother was extremely sick and appeared as though divorced from the living.

The storm lasted three full days. The nights were the worst as sleep was impossible and I was scared out of my wits. How long would this storm last? Would the ship sink? These thoughts were constantly on my mind. America seemed very far away. I was entertained by a friendly crew member, one of the few people still around since most of the passengers were bedridden, so I welcomed his friendship.

The storm abated at last, not immediately, but with each passing hour the ship's relentless motion became more bearable. To my great surprise, the friendly crewmember showed me the bridge where the captain was steering the ship. The skies had cleared with patches of blue ahead. I was amazed at all the dials and gauges. It must have been exciting to have the job of a captain.

The crewmember even showed me the engine room, a noisy, hot place with the smell of oil and smoke. The SS *Drottningholm* was a coal-driven ship, and the immense furnaces were red hot and provided steam to operate the massive engines which turned the propeller shaft. The sound was deafening, and the seamen were sweaty and dirty. It was impossible to talk above the din. My interests in machinery went back to my days with my grandfather in Inkeroinen. You might say that I was in heaven. My new friend spoke Swedish with a strange accent, far different than that of Ryningsnäs. He finally brought me back to my cabin. My mother was still ill and didn't want any food. Hopefully she would feel better for the entry into New York Harbor.

Our cruise became smoother with each passing hour and people began to reappear from their cabins and take gingerly strolls along the promenades. Gordon had recovered at last, and I excitedly relayed my experiences of having seen the bridge, the captain at the helm and, of course, the engine room. He was plainly envious, having missed out on this adventure. The dining room was open for all meals though not as frequented as before. Mother felt a little better, and she even risked a light lunch. The next few days were wonderful, and we were getting more excited about arriving in America and sailing into the largest city in the world.

Mother had gotten a book titled *Kävin tähtilipun maassa*, meaning "I Visited the Country of the Star-Studded Flag," written by a Finnish woman who had toured America and written a detailed account of her travels. This book gave me insight into life in America and I, being an avid reader since the third grade, read this book several times over.

One day we met a Finnish gentleman by the name of Erkki Salonen while in the dining room. He happened to live in Berkeley, California, our destination in America. He spoke English well and offered to help us upon our arrival in New York. He was the most wonderful godsend, as we would have had a rough time trying to find our way around New York City with neither of us knowing English. Having established this contact, Mother's fears were immediately dispelled. I hadn't given it any thought, being a twelve-year-old kid with no worries to speak of.

Touching New Shores

Stamped passport – George and Bertta.

After ten days at sea, the SS *Drottningholm* eased into New York Harbor and passed by the Statue of Liberty. The open decks were filled with passengers, some teary-eyed, others in awe. I was so excited to see all the grandeur of the harbor and the tip of Manhattan with its skyscrapers soaring up to the clouds. (The tallest building in Helsinki in 1947 was the Tower Hotel, a fourteen-story building in the Centrum.) The Hudson River was filled with docks, most of them occupied by cruise ships from many countries. The streets were bustling with automobiles of every make and model, and with taxi cabs, most of them yellow with

187

checkerboard markings. The ship moved at a leisurely pace and the fairytale trip continued. Gosh, this was America, for which we'd been waiting so long.

At last, the ship docked along a lengthy wharf, the Swedish American Line dock. The dockside cranes loomed above, ready to retrieve cargo from the ship's holds. Our cabin was bathed in daylight as the overhead covers were removed. We were led up to the promenade and ushered down the gangplank into a cavernous warehouse. Our newly acquainted friend, Erkki, understood the instructions from the officials and jumped into action, leading us to an area marked by a large letter M intended for families whose last names started with that letter. The baggage followed soon thereafter. I gaped in wonder at all this humanity. I couldn't understand a word and felt so terribly shut out because of it. Mother had not fully recovered from seasickness and was still very weak. Erkki, sizing up the situation, hailed a cab and made arrangements at a nearby hotel so that she would be able to recuperate sufficiently to continue our trip by train to the west coast.

Our hotel was in Manhattan, not far from Rockefeller Center. Erkki had leased a two-bedroom place where Mother would be able to get a much-needed rest on solid ground, as the swaying ship had not been conducive to her overall health. Erkki and I went to investigate the magic of the city. He took me to Rockefeller Center where we rode several express elevators to the uppermost observation point. My ears popped and my stomach screamed as the elevator took off. Everything in America was bigger and faster than in Finland. The view from the roof was indescribably beautiful and the air was crystal clear. Erkki pointed out the Empire

State Building (the tallest structure in the world at that time), the magnificent Central Park in the opposite direction, the Hudson River, from where we had come, and yes, the SS *Drottningholm* still docked at the pier, undoubtedly readying for a return trip to Göteborg. I saw four-engined airplanes flying overhead, which was yet another first. Erkki seemed pleased at my never-ending enthusiasm as it reminded him of his own arrival in America, many years ago.

We walked along Times Square through the busy streets. I wondered how one could cross to the other side of the street, with all the fast-moving traffic. Erkki related a story to me about a man who wanted to cross the street and, upon seeing another man across the way, hollered to him, "How in the world did you get to the other side?" Upon hearing him, the man across the street shouted back, "I was born on this side!" It soon became evident that it was quite easy to cross with the green light. Of course, I had never seen traffic lights in Helsinki, at least not in 1947.

One of the most interesting things happened later in the afternoon. As we strolled down the sidewalk, I stopped to look in the window of a café. To my amazement I saw a glass pot of water boiling over an open flame. This was mindboggling. How could that be? I remember so well when Hanna tried to pour hot coffee into a glass bottle, only to see it shatter from the heat. Yet here, in broad daylight, right before my eyes, this glass pot filled with water was joyously bubbling without breaking. Erkki explained that the glass pot was tempered and wouldn't break from the heat. "Only in America," I managed to utter.

The wonders just kept coming. Two doors down, at another café, I saw another unusual sight. A young lady, dressed in a white uniform, stopped to put white bread slices into a strange machine. The bread began to move upward very slowly, ultimately disappearing from our view. As the bread slices appeared on the other side, they suddenly fell to the tray below, but this time they were brown on both sides. Gee, a magic trick in the middle of the day, I thought. Erkki, noticing my puzzlement, quickly explained that this device was called a toaster. "Okay, then!" I exclaimed. Our bread in Finland was already brown as it was made from rye, and it was firm and impossible to squeeze into a dough ball. The glass pot and toaster lingered in my memory for years to come as the most interesting sights upon my arrival in America.

Mother was beginning to feel stronger. Erkki ordered her dinner which she ate sparingly. Perhaps another day of rest would help. She welcomed the relaxing solitude and urged us to go out later in the evening. Erkki and I strolled down the "Great White Way," as he called it. Movie houses lined both sides of the street, and the myriad of overhead light bulbs glowed brightly over the street below. We went to see a movie and just walked in, right in middle of the show, which seemed extremely strange to me because in Finland one could only enter the theater at the very beginning, and what's more, food and drink were not allowed. Erkki bought a bag of popcorn, another first for me, and as I bit into it, the corn just seemed to disappear into thin air. As for the movie, I couldn't understand it all. It took place in the desert in some far distant land where there were camels, horses, and people dressed like Arabs.

It was fun being out late. The lit-up streets made it seem like the middle of a sunny day. Neon signs were flashing everywhere, and thousands of light bulbs blinked, giving off a lot of heat. Well-dressed people were bustling here and there, and I saw different people, Black and Asian, that I'd never seen before. I heard a multitude of languages spoken, none of them familiar. I had never seen so many people milling around. The street noise was deafening. Erkki patiently helped me with my numerous questions which just kept coming. It was disorienting to suddenly be moved from the small city of Helsinki into the world's largest city in such a short time. The sudden changes were simply astonishing, more than my young mind could possibly handle. Erkki suggested that we return to the hotel for a good night's sleep and I happily obliged.

The following morning found Mother feeling quite chipper. She was hungry and we had a sturdy breakfast in a nearby café. She was anxious to continue our trip as we were still days away from Berkeley, where her sister Alma had lived since emigrating from Finland years before. I had no comprehension of the size of America. Living in Finland and Sweden had given me some understanding of the sizes of countries, but I simply couldn't fathom the idea that it would take several days to reach our destination.

The Train Trip to California

Erkki hailed a yellow taxicab to bring us to the New York Central Railroad Station. It was a colossal building, and inside were many sleek trains that were vastly unlike the steam locomotives I was familiar with. We boarded the train and were helped up the steps by a porter in a white jacket and a bright red cap with a shiny black visor. He smiled at us, and his gold-capped teeth glittered in the sunshine. Our coach was furnished with comfortable seats and the ample-sized windows allowed an unobstructed view of the scenery. The train began its imperceptible movement and soon slid out of the station. We gathered speed and slowly left New York City behind. I remained glued to the window, absorbing the magical scenery of America. It was hard to believe that we had finally arrived in the greatest country in the world. We traveled through Pennsylvania and Ohio with their rolling green hills and farmlands. The train made a few stops in the major cities, but for the most part it sped along the smooth tracks almost noiselessly. I experienced another first as we ate our dinner in the dining car. The food was well-prepared and tasty. White-coated waiters served the meals on spotless linen tablecloths. It made me feel like an important person and I was so glad to be in America.

I wished that my friend Timo could have been here to share my wonderful experiences. I'm so glad that mother had made the decision to come to America, though I don't really know what prompted her to do so. Perhaps it was the knowledge that life would never get better in Finland, no matter how hard she had to work.

Soon we would travel through Michigan. Erkki told us that all automobiles were built in this great state. We soon approached Chicago, where we could see the skyline with its skyscrapers as well as Lake Michigan. Erkki had reserved a hotel room for us as we were going to have to kill some time that evening. We leased a cab for the afternoon so we could see the sights of Chicago and we drove up and down the majestic Lake Michigan shoreline with its world-renowned hotels. Erkki told us that Chicago had been dubbed the Windy City due to the steady winds blowing inland from the lake. To me, the lake looked like an ocean, but I was slowly getting accustomed to the idea that everything in America was indeed grand.

We were treated to a trip to the aquarium near the lakeside, which was housed in a beautiful large building and contained fish and sea creatures collected from various parts of the world. I was so taken with the sleek sharks behind plate-glass windows, swimming around with their mouths partly open and looking ahead with their hypnotizing black eyes. We saw octopuses, electric eels that resembled sea snakes, sea horses, and tropical fish of every conceivable shape and color. We spent several hours at the aquarium and Erkki had us try hotdogs for a late lunch. Mother wasn't too fond of them, but I wolfed mine down with a bottle of Coca Cola. I had never seen a hotdog in my short lifetime, and I welcomed this new treat.

We spent a quiet evening in the hotel and continued our journey the following morning on another streamlined train bound for Berkeley, California. This train took us through Wisconsin, Minnesota, and South Dakota, where we saw the Badlands, an unforgettable sight of jagged, pastel-colored rock formations. Nature had formed these rocky hills over thousands of years, with wind and rain having taken a big role in their development.

The train turned southward, and we traveled by the Great Salt Lake late at night under a full moon. Erkki seemed to know so much about the American scenery. As we rode through Nevada, we saw miles and miles of desert. Erkki told us that the city of Reno was frequented by visitors from all over America and that most of them lost bundles of money at the gaming tables, though occasionally a lucky gambler would hit a jackpot and go home with a small fortune. Only in America!

We were approaching the Sierra Nevada Mountain range. To cross these high and winding mountains, the train was equipped with two enormous locomotives that had the strength to haul the long passenger train up the slopes. The train crossed the Sierras on curvy tracks, and we could see the locomotive in the front and the very last car in the rear of the train simultaneously as it rounded the bends. The mountains were steep, dropping into deep gorges, and we crossed over several bridges which spanned one drop-off after another. This was a fascinating leg of the trip.

Bertta and George.

Arrival in Berkeley

We finally reached the flat lands of California. Erkki told us that California was known as the Golden State and he told us the story of the Gold Rush of 1849 and how they discovered the precious metal at Sutter's Fort. He also told us about the two famous suspension bridges in San Francisco. I couldn't wait to see this famous city. Arriving in California seemed so magical, and our expectations were at a pinnacle. Mother had received many letters and photos from her sister Alma, as well as a portrait of her with her husband, George, a good-looking man of whom Alma seemed proud. George was a stage director and had produced numerous plays. Alma's photos depicted a beautiful white home with red steps and flowers that bloomed even in the winter. We were nearing our destination, and we could hardly wait for our arrival.

Our trip from Helsinki to Berkeley took twenty days, ten of those onboard the SS *Drottningholm*. The *City of San Francisco*, our aptly named train, pulled up to the Berkeley station, a petite California-style building unlike the giant edifices of Chicago and New York City. We felt our travel-tired bodies re-energize as we excitedly walked down the station steps. Searching for familiar faces, we saw Alma and George Niemi and their baby Denise waiting on the platform, though we didn't recognize the man standing a little further back. Mother hadn't seen her sister since she had left Finland many years before, and they hugged one another for a long time and shed tears of happiness. Alma also hugged and kissed me, which made me feel uncomfortable as public displays of affection were not the norm in Finland or Sweden. I was so embarrassed and hoped that no one had seen it. George greeted us with a warm handshake while holding his baby girl. He then introduced us to Kalle Maki, Aunt Aino's husband. Mother had known Aunt Aino as a child in Finland. Kalle had volunteered to drive his car to the railroad station. Wow, he owned a car, and an Oldsmobile to say the least! No one we had known in Finland owned an automobile. Our baggage arrived while we were busy greeting one another and we all managed to fit in Kalle's car for the ride home.

Alma spoke a type of Finnish that was mixed with a lot of English words. It was called Finglish, a form of Finnish which had been adopted by many Finns living in the United States. At first, we found it difficult to understand but with time, it became more comprehensible. Unfortunately, it didn't take Mother very long before she adopted her own version of Finglish. I disliked speaking like this and fought it valiantly, forcing myself to speak the Finnish that I had learned in school. My decision to use the "correct" Finnish proved to be advantageous in the future. "Don't forget your Finnish heritage!" rang loudly in my mind. These words were etched in my memory, and I had promised my friends that I would not forget them.

Mother and Alma were busy chatting while Kalle drove us through Berkeley to the Niemis' home, a tiny three-room, wooden-frame structure situated in the rear of a small lot on Curtis Street. It was not the same house we had seen in her photos. Upon asking, Alma explained that she had lived there during her previous marriage which had ended in divorce some five years ago. The Niemis' home consisted of a living room, bedroom, and small kitchen with a stove, refrigerator, eating area, and a washer and dryer. It seemed large to us. We had not had a refrigerator nor a washer and dryer in Finland, and in our minds it seemed luxurious. Their home also had one bathroom equipped with a four-legged bathtub and shower. Though impressive, it was not the typical home I had seen in American movies.

Alma seated us in their living room, and we had a chance to talk about our long journey. She was filled with questions about our trip. How had we possibly fared in New York City? Mother told her how we had met a wonderful Finnish gentleman, miraculously from Berkeley, while on board the SS *Drottningholm*. He had offered his assistance to navigate the big city and came to mother's aid during her illness. When Alma heard his name, she was quite astonished and told us that she knew him. He happened to be a very influential member of the Finnish Kaleva Hall and was considered very well off. He resided in the Berkeley Hills, a fashionable section of the city. Erkki Salonen was well-known in the Finnish circles, and we had been fortunate in benefitting from his friendship and generosity. We would not have made it to our destination nearly as easily without his help and we remained thankful for his assistance. Alma seemed envious of our relationship upon hearing of our connection to Erkki, and by suddenly changing the subject it became clear to us that she no longer wanted to discuss our stay in New York and Chicago.

Alma planned a welcoming dinner for us the next day since it was a weekend. She invited Kalle and Aino, and Mini and Fred, who lived in San Francisco, so we could meet them firsthand. Alma was an accomplished cook; in her youth she had worked as a house cleaner and helped the kitchen staff prepare dinners for well-to-do families. This occasion allowed her to display her cooking skills by preparing an extravagant, sit-down meal, and it promised to be just that. She opened the dining room table and put out place settings for eight people. The living room, being small, was nearly filled by the expanded table. Fred and Mini arrived with their family dog, a black and white mix, friendly by nature but somewhat wary of strangers.

Kalle and Aino met us with loving greetings and Mother was visibly moved to see her two American aunts. A third aunt, Helen, was unable to visit because she was busy playing the ponies, her number one favorite pastime. She lived on the San Francisco Peninsula and worked as a full-time maid in an upscale home. She had remained single her entire life, and her interest in horse racing was legendary. Once in a while Lady Luck took a shine on her, and so re-energized, she carted her hard-earned money back to the racetrack in the hopes of hitting it rich again.

While Alma prepared the feast, George, the bartender, prepared mixed drinks for the adults. The day was warm and sunny, allowing us to congregate outside in the grassy yard between the little white house and George's vegetable garden. The whole yard was surrounded by a sturdy hedge which offered privacy from the sidewalk and street. We had a lot to talk about, though Mini's husband, Fred, did not speak Finnish. He was of Italian descent and spoke with a deep voice. Kalle liked his drinks and after having a few extra rounds, became quite jolly. In fact, he jokingly shared some of his drink with Fred's dog, which I thought to be mean-spirited. The poor animal became slightly intoxicated which caused a heated altercation between the two men.

Dinnertime brought us inside to the fancy table with its bounty. There was ham, scalloped potatoes, several vegetable dishes, and a Jello salad. Even though we filled our plates with care, they were still overflowing. As we began dining, it soon became apparent that Mother and I hadn't acquired a taste for many of the foods. We had never seen Jello salad, squash dishes, asparagus, and other delicacies. We did not want to appear unappreciative, but we found it difficult to finish everything on our plates. Unfortunately, Aunt Alma was visibly disappointed and took this as an insult. We were apologetic and tried to offer explanations for our behavior, but it seemed to cast a pall over the dinner table. We hoped that she would overcome her displeasure and perhaps in time she would understand. We would, ultimately, come to like all these wonderful dishes.

We were still tired from our travels and fervently hoped that we wouldn't have to spend too much time living here. The quarters were tight with five people living under the roof of this tiny home. Our welcome slowly eroded and we understandably wanted to find a place of our own. It was very confining sleeping on the studio couch. It also became increasingly more difficult to share one bathroom. The small bedroom was cramped with the baby's crib and a couple of dressers, which made it difficult for George to get up early in the morning and find space to prepare for the day. He worked as a welder in the shipyards, which surprised us because we had pictured him as a professional man. Almas had referred to him as a "director" in her letters to us. Life in America was turning out to be quite different from what we had expected, and it was paramount that we move on. Mother wanted to find a job as soon as possible in order to chart her own life. School would not begin for yet another month, so at least we had a little extra time for planning.

Betrayal and Moving On

Mother was anxious to get to her trunk and extract the funds that her friend Kalle had so ingeniously concealed within the walls. The Swedish kronor would easily be converted into American dollars. George had promised to help us after work. It was Mother's intention to pay Alma for what we hoped would be a brief stay at their home. We were thankful that we had the opportunity to lodge there, but we were so crowded and didn't want to overstay our welcome.

Upon his return from work George looked exhausted and grimy. His job was not an easy one and it required physical strength under less-than-perfect circumstances. His clothing had small burns and his face and arms were scarred from the red-hot sparks emitted during the welding process. He seemed extra tired this evening as he took a shower, changed his clothes and gave his daughter a quick bath, something that Alma seemed to expect of him. She spent most of the day chatting with Mother, smoking one cigarette after another and enjoying her little "mickeys," sips of Muscatel wine.

Alma warmed up the leftovers from the previous day and we sat down for a quick meal in preparation for the opening of the trunk. George and I dragged the trunk into the living room, and he got his tools from the rear shed. We unscrewed the metal angles from the four edges and George, with the aid of a hammer and chisel, began to chip away at the edges, soon finding the locations that concealed the money. Mother was extremely excited and waited with bated breath, as this was her security bundle. She had sold her apartment and all her earthly belongings, and she needed these funds to start a new life in America. However, with each chip of the chisel, we soon found, to our horror, that what should have been a small fortune turned out to be a few rolled-up Swedish bills. There was no fortune, there was no money. Mother was devastated and burst out crying. Kalle had bilked her of her veritable fortune, and he was back in Finland, safe from prosecution, in the knowledge that he could enjoy the stolen money. This was horrible. Devastatingly horrible.

George and Alma were speechless as well. Alma seemed to have her doubts regarding Mother's story and thought it seemed far-fetched and ludicrous. Mother's tears turned first into amazement and then into anger, not believing what she was hearing. The look of disbelief on her sister's face spoke volumes. The situation grew tense as the two got into a heated argument. I was sick to my stomach from the show of utter distrust by my aunt, and I ran outside, though I was completely unfamiliar with the neighborhood. I felt so lost and lonely. The shouting continued in the small bungalow. At last, George was able to calm the flaring tempers and reason with the two women. He was visibly angry with Alma for not believing her sister.

The fact of the matter was that Kalle had taken the trunk to a local furniture repair shop across the street from our flat, and since neither my mother nor I had been present while Kalle hid the money, he had the perfect opportunity to plot his embezzlement scheme. Mother had placed all her trust in her friend, and she was heartbroken to realize that she had no money with which to cover our temporary lodging. She insisted on looking for work and asked her sister to help her learn how to navigate the public transportation system and to speak on her behalf to a prospective employer.

Mother had become highly skilled as a furrier and was equally competent as a seamstress in the fur trade. Her skills became another sore point for Alma, since her own jobs in the United States had been mostly limited to housekeeping. With Alma's assistance, Mother got a job in North Berkeley working for a boutique called Furs by Bruce. Mother was no stranger to public transportation, and she thus began her very first job in America. She was an immediate hit with her boss and seemed to be on her way up. She soon found an even better job working for the luxury department store I. Magnin in San Francisco. She was well-regarded in the fur coat department and was considered just as gifted as any of the men who worked there, though, being a woman, she did not receive the same wages.

Our close quarters were partly responsible for the many disagreements between the two sisters. It seemed that nothing we did pleased Alma, and it became increasingly difficult to live with the Niemis. Mother finally decided to part ways and move to Aunt Aino's home until we could find a place of our own. It was relatively easy to pack up our few belongings and ride the city bus to their home. We were given our own bedroom and since the kitchen was spacious, Mother spent most of the days working. Though we didn't yet have the means to move into our own quarters, Kalle and Aino understood our situation and were more than glad to help us out. Aino, while sickly, was congenial and easy to get along with, and Kalle was fun to be around, so we hit it off nicely. We would go to a nearby Finnish sauna where we met other Finnish old-timers. Kalle drove his Oldsmobile and I got to sit in the front seat. I watched him drive the car and thought to myself how easy it seemed to drive. Well, maybe someday? Kalle was an accomplished carpenter and he pointed out many buildings around Berkeley that he had helped to construct.

Learning Again

Finnish-Swedish baths. (George is several years older here).

It was time for school to start. I had completed the fifth grade in Helsinki, but I was placed into the fifth grade again until I could learn the language. I found school to be quite easy, as we had covered the same ground earlier in Finland. Fractions and geography were no problem whatsoever, but the language was very difficult at first. I tried speaking both Finnish and Swedish but got no reaction. Initially I was somewhat of a curiosity to the other students, until I was lucky enough to meet a boy named Craig Mortenson. He took an avid interest in me, teaching me English words each day by pointing to objects and then sounding them out. He was friendly, and extremely patient and helpful. It didn't take very long until I was conversing with my other classmates. My schoolteacher was very amiable, and she encouraged me to draw pictures, many of which she put on the wall. I loved to draw pictures of ships, airplanes, tall skyscrapers – all the things I had seen on our journey to Berkeley.

Craig also helped get me a job as a newspaper boy. At first, I carried my papers on foot, then later roller skates, enabling me to deliver my papers more quickly. The Mortensons lent me money to buy a bicycle and I was on my way to becoming one of the best paper boys in our district. I managed to repay them for the bicycle within a short time.

It didn't take long before I was promoted to the sixth grade. I liked my friends and soon fit in quite well with my new classmates. I was infatuated with a girl named Georgia who had straight, jet black hair and blue eyes and lived across the street from us. She was the prettiest girl I had ever seen, and we walked home together every day.

We had been living with Kalle and Aunt Aino for some time until Aino became quite ill and had to go to the hospital, so Mother and I had to move out. I would really miss Georgia. We moved back to Alma and George's home until we could find a place of our own. At first, things went smoothly, but it wasn't long before Mother and Alma were feuding again. One night they got into a fierce argument. Tempers flared, strong language erupted, and in desperation, I walked over to the Mortensons' home. At least I had made some friends which allowed me to get away for a while.

When I returned home later that night, I found a police car parked in the driveway. I hid in the tall bushes surrounding the house and discovered that Alma had notified the police that I was missing. I remained in the bushes until the police car left. Mother had gone somewhere as well but returned later in the evening. She summoned me and told me that we were moving that very evening. She had found a nearby house where we could stay with a young Finnish couple who had two little kids. We were to share their home by subletting a little bedroom in the rear of the house. We could use their kitchen and bathroom and had entry from a rear porch. It was not an ideal place, but it was more private than Alma's home and at least the arguments came to a halt. Mother continued to work in San Francisco, and I was able to complete the sixth grade at Jefferson Grammar School.

My paper route was very close to our new temporary home. I learned how to solicit new customers and I got more than my share of new subscriptions. These helped me win prizes and work my way up the ladder as a newspaper carrier. I earned about $28 a month and opened a bank account nearby. Things were beginning to look brighter and brighter. I received many tips from my customers for being courteous and for my prompt deliveries. I volunteered to carry other paperboys' routes when they were ill or on vacation. I earned extra money this way and I also canvassed their routes for new customers, often getting new subscriptions for them. I got the credit for the new customers and even collected their routes during their absence.

Our living arrangement went smoothly at first, but the weekends didn't fare as well. The man of the house tended to drink, and he was a veritable womanizer who seemed to attract beautiful women. He often came home late and started arguments with his wife, sometimes slapping her around. One night she ran into our bedroom to escape the beatings and crawled under our bed. He knocked on our door, but we wouldn't let him in. It was a little scary living like this. After all, this was America, and it was nothing like I had imagined. Mother continued to look for other places to live and after searching for several months she finally found a small, two-bedroom home to rent on Delaware Street. At last, we were alone, with no one arguing, and we finally felt safe.

Mother continued to work in San Francisco at I. Magnin, and I started at Burbank Junior High School and continued to carry the Oakland Tribune. At last, we were independent in America. I liked my paper route and I found that by working hard and even working overtime, life in this country would eventually pay off. My English skills continued to improve, and Mother started taking evening English classes. We didn't see Alma and George very often, realizing that it was better to stay away and avoid arguments. Aunt Aino's health got progressively worse, and she sadly passed away, leaving Kalle a widower.

Time passed and I progressed well in school. My mother opened a savings account and continued to prosper as a furrier. Our new life in America had begun with a few setbacks, but we both agreed that our lives were going to be wonderful.

Scandinavia Revisited

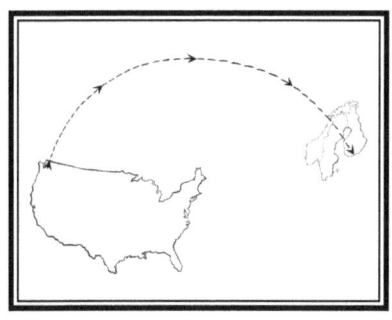

The Return

Twenty-eight years after leaving Ryningsnäs, Sweden, I returned to this picturesque village accompanied by my wife Evelyn and our three young daughters. We found ourselves in this small Swedish village, a necessary side trip while visiting Finland and Scandinavia in the summer of 1972. Why so necessary? Well, I had a remarkably strong yearning to return to my roots.

We were traveling by car, a little red Volkswagen which we had leased in Stockholm. Somehow, we comfortably fit in this little car with all our luggage and souvenirs purchased during our travels. Our five-week-long voyage brought us to Ryningsnäs, to bring closure to my young life during the Finnish-Russian war.

Our very first stop was the little railroad station where I had witnessed the incredible chamber pot caper. My wife Evie and our daughters finally had the opportunity to see this station house of which they had heard so much during my storytelling sessions. Surprisingly, the station had barely changed after all these years. It was still there as if waiting for me to validate this story which happened so many years

211

ago. The village store was also there, though it was bigger than before. The hitching post, where I had secured my horse, Fia, was no longer there. We entered the little station house with its wooden benches and barred ticket window. In my mind I could still visualize the event. My girls were fascinated by the old story and this visit brought credence to the event.

After lingering there for a few minutes we continued our journey to my home in the village that was once governed by the stately agronomer. I had no trouble finding it. It was dreamlike to be able to return to my past, as if traveling by time machine. The Persson's home and the creamery were still intact, as were the large barns. Evie commented on the farm structures, realizing at last that my descriptions of them were quite accurate. Somehow, she had pictured them to be a lot smaller, thinking that in a child's memory things usually seemed larger than in real life. To our surprise, we found that this village had been converted into a tree farm and was no longer used to raise horses and cows. The farm buildings served as a museum of sorts. Magically, everything in the village seemed intact, as if waiting for my return home. Aunt Sigrid and Uncle Pelle no longer lived in the creamery, and eerily, we saw no one in the village. The fields, now lined with young trees, were no longer the grassy feeding grounds for livestock.

Eagerly, I showed my family the various parts of the farm. The village blacksmith building was still there, and I could hardly wait to show them the agronomer's mansion. However, to my big surprise, when we got to the site of the mansion on the hill it was gone. No mansion, not even the very foundation. It was as though it had never been there. What a disappointment. I still have photos of this magnificent three-story building, a castle-like structure. It had been the very heart and soul of the village. Now in its place was a grassy knoll filled with various kinds of trees.

We continued our journey to my country schoolhouse, wondering what we would find there. A dirt road led us outside the farm buildings, snaking its way through the forest. We came to a little wooden bridge spanning the railroad track. I spotted a little sign by the bridge but couldn't fully decipher its message. I believe it warned that the bridge was unsafe for automobiles. Not knowing any better, we crossed the bridge regardless and fortunately, it held our little car. After all, the honeybee, according to the calculations and analyses of engineers, cannot fly its heavy body with its tiny wings, but the bee doesn't know that and continues to fly to its heart's content from flower to flower. The old road merged with the main highway, and we drove on. Soon we turned off onto another little dirt road which, if my memory served me right, led to my schoolhouse. Slowly we crept down the small hill and to my pleasant surprise we found the ivy-covered structure. The tiny schoolyard was deserted except for a tall, elderly man who was busy lowering the blue and yellow Swedish flag. He didn't see us driving in, nor did he hear us approach. Oh my, could it be? Could it possibly be my third-grade teacher, Mr. Bernhard Morstam? I had previously described him to my wife and the similarity was uncanny. I stopped our car, got out, and walked toward the gentleman. His back was turned toward me as he lowered the flag and was folding it carefully according to Swedish custom. I remained silent, not wanting to startle him. Slowly he turned around, looked at me curiously at first, but then suddenly uttered, "Matti Makela, is it you?" After twenty-eight years he remembered me and recognized me as a grown man. Now, how incredible is that? It turned out to be Mr. Morstam after all. My, what a surprise. I turned around and looked at my wife and girls who were still in the car. Their faces said it all, such astounded looks. My former teacher gave me a hug to beat all hugs and yelled to his wife to come and meet me. His wife came running toward us with an amazed look on her face and I was met with another loving hug. My family came running from the car, also with amazed looks on their faces. I tried my best to communicate with the Morstams in the little Swedish that I could remember. As the story unfolded, they told us that they no longer lived there but had moved to Målilla. In fact, the school had been closed for several years. They had come to this seldom-used schoolhouse to meet with other retired villagers for an afternoon get-together. Our unscheduled stop had found them there strictly by luck. The Morstams invited us to visit them at their home. Of course, we accepted gladly. Upon inquiring about the whereabouts of Hilda Edstrom, my first-grade teacher, we found that she lived nearby. We promised that we would visit them later in the day, but first I wanted to visit Hilda.

We found her little cottage, and Hilda, now in her twilight years, invited us in. I do believe she remembered who I was, but I wasn't completely sure. We visited for a short time, during which she alternated between long periods of silence and coherency. We managed to take a few photos with her, then we departed. I hoped that she somehow remembered me.

Later that afternoon we drove to the Morstams' home. When I left Sweden in 1944, the Morstams had six children. Now they had nine, and all of them were teachers. Fortunately, my friend Per and his sister Karin, whom I had also known as a child, also came to visit their parents. Their English was impeccable; how fortunate for me. They were more than happy to translate our conversation to their parents as we reminisced about our childhood days. It wasn't long before Mrs. Morstam, according to Swedish custom, prepared us a sumptuous smorgasbord. There were tiny meatballs, thinly sliced beef, three kinds of cheese, and those delicious cream-filled pastries. The steaming coffee topped off this totally unexpected feast.

The Morstams inquired about our lives in America, my schooling, and my occupation as a mechanical engineer at Boeing. Our daughters were the center of attention, and each girl was presented with a Swedish keepsake to take home. With smiles on their faces, they gracefully accepted the gifts. We were so proud of their behavior and with the compliments regarding our children's upbringing.

I was anxiously hoping that they would know the whereabouts of my foster parents. They were happy to relate that the Perssons had moved to Oskarshamn, and they just happened to have their address on hand. Aunt Sigrid and Uncle Pelle had two daughters, both born after my departure. I could hardly contain my happiness upon hearing these wonderful words. I wanted so much for my family to meet these amazing people. We bade farewell to the Morstams and departed for Oskarshamn after asking them to refrain from calling ahead; I wanted our meeting to be a surprise.

We arrived in Oskarshamn in the late afternoon where we found Klokkarbakken Gatan, or "Watchmaker's Street."

While driving slowly down their street, excitedly looking for their house number, I saw an elderly, white-haired man standing in middle of the street. I stopped the car and rolled down the window to ask him for directions. All at once, two arms shot inside the car and enveloped my shoulders as the man called me by name again and again. Yes, it was Uncle Pelle! He looked slightly familiar, though age had whitened his jet-black hair, and he was no longer the tall man I knew from my childhood. He urged me to park the car and he literally pulled us into his modest home. Aunt Sigrid met us inside and she hugged me for the longest time. With great pride, I introduced my wife and daughters to the Perssons. Uncle Pelle made a quick phone call and invited his two daughters, Monica and Helena, who arrived in no time. Each of them spoke effortless English, of which I was so thankful since I had forgotten the Swedish language. As I listened to my foster parents speak in their native tongue, I was able to understand some words here and there. Helena gladly translated back and forth. They were so happy to finally have the opportunity to meet me because throughout their lives they had heard so much about me. Uncle Pelle asked me, jokingly, if I remembered burning down the forest, and upon hearing his question I couldn't help but blush ever so slightly, hoping that no one had noticed. But I was glad to report that I never again started any destructive fires, with or without my spyglass.

It didn't take Aunt Sigrid long to set up another smorgasbord. Everything was delicious, even though we had gorged ourselves at the Morstams'. We reminisced about old times in Ryningsnäs, and I found that they had been forewarned of our arrival after all. Our visit had been so very special, and the Morstams just couldn't contain themselves. No wonder Uncle Pelle was waiting for us in the middle of the street. What a remarkable reunion, first in Målilla and now here in Oskarshamn.

We conversed for hours and talked about our lives in the state of Washington, our current home. Their modest home was too small to house our family of five, so Uncle Pelle brought us to a nearby hotel. As I drove our little red Volkswagen, Uncle Pelle walked next to our car. He found us a nice hotel not far from their home. We thanked him for the wonderful meal and the get-together. We were so exhausted from our drive and from our unexpected visits with my first-grade teacher, Hilda Ekstrom, with the Morstams, and finally with my foster parents. This was the Mother of all Reunions, considering that we had literally stumbled upon my third-grade teacher who made this all possible.

The following morning after a delicious breakfast, we joined the Perssons for a walk. We strolled to the waterfront and miraculously, the world's longest wooden bench was still there, just as I remembered it from nearly thirty years before. Helena accompanied us as our translator. It was wonderful to re-live the past. The long docks were unchanged with the hustle and bustle of life at sea. Ships were being unloaded and reloaded as we sat on this famous bench. I told my daughters that, when I was their age, I had sat in the same spot where they were now sitting. Uncle Pelle and Aunt Sigrid told us over and over how they had enjoyed our surprise visit, and they were sad to see us go later that afternoon. Our reunion had come to an end, and we finally left with tears in our eyes.

I will always keep the memory of my wonderful Swedish family in my heart. In the process of writing this memoir I know that many moments were forgotten over time. Nevertheless, those early childhood experiences helped mold and form me into the man I would become.

Stockholm, Sweden — 2023

Afterword

By Carol Makela

As I've come to the end of this process, of reading, re-reading, and editing over and over and over, I find myself at a stuck point. How to end. How to summarize. How to wrap up a life that, itself, ended far sooner than any of us could have imagined. My father lost consciousness shortly after bypass surgery. He did not die immediately; rather, he entered an unconscious state from which the doctors told us he was not expected to recover. For nearly two long weeks, the immediate family gathered to discuss options, and all eventually agreed to pull life support. Dad would never have acquiesced to life in a vegetative state. His abrupt death caught us all off-guard. It seemed he had so much more life; that we all had so much more time to spend with him. His memoir was cut short before it got a chance to be shared with the wider world. I was unaware, at the time of his death, that he had been writing a memoir at all.

Traveling down the path of memory brought deep feelings to consciousness. How might my re-visioning of these memories be affected by my own unconscious traumas? In asking these questions I began to explore the science and psychology of epigenetics and found that "exposure to adversities such as war . . . can lead to enduring changes in the next generation" and that there is an "important role of the father in transmitting the potentially adverse effects of early trauma and war".[8] At first glance, this seems like dark news; that we are all genetically programmed by the traumas and experiences of our ancestors. However, research suggests that this transmission of trauma is not biologically transmitted, but passed on genetically via our environment and specifically, from "our perception of the environment".[9] I have come to believe that we might bypass the early programming that occurred in our intimate family environments by forming new habits that will override negative family patterns. Perhaps through revisiting our own pasts and those of our ancestors we can create new patterns for our lives and for those who will come after.

At the time of my father's death and throughout the following decade, my personal world was unstable as I struggled to gain the means to support my small family, as my grandmother Bertta had also done as a single parent. The global slowdown during Covid allowed me the time and mental space to earn a master's degree, and to eventually pick up my father's memoir with the intention of organizing,

[8] Ramo, F. L., Schneider, A., Wilker, S., & Kolassa, I. (2015). Epigenetic alterations associated with war trauma and childhood maltreatment. Behavioral Sciences & the Law, 33(5), 701–721. https://doi-org.pgi.idm.oclc.org/10.1002/bsl.2200

[9] London Real (Host). (2017, August, 25). Bruce Lipton - biology of belief [Podcast]. https://londonreal.tv/bruce-lipton-biology-of-belief/

editing, writing an introduction, and publishing it for the wider world. I kickstarted the final writing process by sending myself on a journey of outer exploration and inner curiosity – I booked a trip for the summer of 2023 during which I would finally bring this tale to a close.

My journey into the past began with a two-week jaunt through the Baltic States of Lithuania, Latvia, and Estonia. The final leg was a ferry crossing from Tallinn to Helsinki during which I spent most of the two-hour trip on the top deck, outdoors, dreaming toward Finland. I scribbled in my journal,

Skyline of Tallinn fades away, embark on the Baltic Sea
Gray and blue, seagulls, voices in varied tongues
Land masses float past, or am I floating?
Moving toward the Motherland
Emotions rolling between gut, throat, memory.

My father describes entering the south harbor of Helsinki as he returned from his three years as a foster child in Sweden. As we made our way into port I kept a lookout for the Church of Finland with its star-studded dome, the Russian Orthodox church, the President's Palace and the open-air Farmer's Market. Swept up in nostalgia, tears arose as the city of Helsinki came into view. Stepping onto Finnish land, I felt like I had arrived home. Some members from my Baltics tour group commented that I seemed somehow radiant. Even though I'd never been to Helsinki except as a five-year-old child, this place felt familiar. I looked forward to formally ending the group tour and making my way on my own.

Glancing back through my travel journal, I had made an entry a day or two before flying across the Atlantic. It begins with a passage by Ginette Paris, a depth psychologist and author whose writing I'd become familiar with during my graduate studies. She writes, "There is no need to travel to revisit the house of our childhood. It cannot be found in a geographical place, only in ourselves, far deep instead of far away".[10] I *had* traveled quite far away from my home and did not know what to expect as I began this portion of my journey into memory and the past. In my journal I asked myself what it means to re-visit memories of our ancestors; is it possible to experience a memory in my ancestral DNA? Would the smell of the harbor, the song of a bird, the breeze in my hair, trip a wire of memory deeply mined inside my psyche? Could I begin to form new patterns for my life as I took a conscious dive into perceptions of the past?

After settling into an economy hotel in the center of Helsinki, I opened Google Maps and set out on foot for Töölö, the neighborhood where Dad lived with his mother for three years before sailing for America. I had a photo of him standing in front of his apartment building, and while I did see similarities in architecture, I could not find the exact address. As I now wandered, cell phone in pocket, I let intuition guide me and found myself at the base of "the big rock." I vaguely remember being here when I was five years old, and it appears in *The Spyglass* as a favorite hangout place for my then near-adolescent father and his friend Timo. I climbed to the top of the steepest hill and sat down among wildflowers and insects, imagining all the people

---

[10] Paris, G. (2018). Pagan Grace: Dionysos, Hermes, and Goddess Memory in Daily Life. United States: Spring Publications.

who have walked, played, daydreamed, or fallen in love on this spot, upon these same stones, among these trees. At the bottom of the rock across a path I came upon a church with its cemetery and a woman laying flowers on a grave. It was Sunday and there were families gathered in the entry and children laughing and playing. As I passed by the edges, I heard a hymn drifting from the interior of the church. A wave of feeling washed over me and, in my bones, I knew that my connection with rock, sky, and tree had found a voice in music. That familiar sensation I associate with sacred places welled up inside and I paused on the path, willing memory to capture the moment.

Several days later I boarded an intercity train from Helsinki Central Station bound for Turku, the same route that my father and grandmother took more than seven decades before as they embarked on their journey to America. What was once a four-hour train ride now speeds by in under two hours, and while much of the landscape is still forested with luminescent birch trees, there is far less farmland and more evidence of industrialism. Turku is located on the southwest coast of Finland and is a main port for sailings to Stockholm. I had several hours before the Viking ship would depart so I found a grassy spot just outside Turku Castle and passed the time reading and imagining into the evenings' passage to Sweden. We sailed out of Turku at 7:30pm while the sky was still lit by the late-summer sun. I hightailed it to the buffet where mountains of mashed potatoes and Swedish meatballs sent my senses into culinary glee. Carrying my tray to a table by the window I couldn't stop giggling at the massive portions on my plate. It was a heavenly feast.

Taking a walk on the top deck of the ship I scanned the passing archipelago, keeping an eye out for the "red-painted houses with white trim around the windows". A storm blew in from the south and while most of the passengers ran for cover, I stayed on deck with the lashing wind and rain. Laughter arose from my deepest depths as lightning crisscrossed the darkening sky. Horizontal torrents swooshed across the deck and the setting sun was pale orange, hovering just above the horizon. The storm quickly passed and the slowly fading summer light lingered for hours.

I was awakened early the next morning by the announcement of our arrival in Stockholm harbor. Chill rain greeted us and would not abate for most of my three days in the Swedish capital. Dashing out to museums during the day, I spent the rest of my time at the writing desk in my hotel. One evening I narrated the pieces I'd written up to this point, out loud, to my father, and I told him about all the places I'd been on this trip. I walked to the window and looked out at darkening sky and falling rain and as I did, tears welled up in torrents. I scribbled in my journal, *It's no surprise that it's been raining here non-stop.*

When I arrived back in Finland I took another train north for Vaasa, the region of my maternal ancestors. I had booked several nights in a hotel that promised a quiet atmosphere and saunas. Having grown up with the sauna as a regular ritual, I have missed this deeply Finnish experience over the years. The hotel was sparsely occupied since the summer season was wrapping up, so every night I had the women's sauna all to myself.

I sit and feel the sweat bead down my face. Darkness. Heat.
When I open my eyes I see my bare legs, my crossed feet.
Another ancestral memory arises.
Me – someone else – also perched on a cedar sauna bench --
Absorbing steam, releasing sorrows.

In the solitary space of the sauna, in my ancestral country of Finland, I could feel a balancing of opposites within myself. Sorrow and joy travel the path together. I can develop new patterns as simple as breathing; new habits as ancient as gratitude.

On my final evening in Helsinki, while re-reading the opening section of my father's text, I noticed that he referred to the street he lived on with his mother and aunt Sylvi. I opened Google Maps to find that it was just blocks from my hotel. I threw on a coat and found my way there, to 'Malminkatu.' Not knowing the address of their apartment, I nonetheless found the street. Imagination kicked in as I pictured this place during the winter of 1939. It was already dark and there were few streetlights. I stood on the street corner, gazing upward, hearing the wail of planes overhead and feeling the panic and dread of mothers and children fleeing to safety. I realized then that my own journey had been made in reverse. I had found my way back, counterclockwise, to the start of the story as I physically ended where my father's journey began, on a simple street in Helsinki.

We are all creatures of time and place and memory. My father wrote of his early life in wartime Finland and the Swedish countryside, and he carried a frugality into many aspects of his adult life. He was conscientious of utility bills, often telling us kids to "put on a parka" when we complained about our cold house in winter. My mother shopped at discount grocery stores, and we didn't match our peers in the latest fashions. My parents' lifestyle became more lavish as they aged, certainly a result of living in the most consumption-driven, materialistic culture that has ever existed: post-war, twentieth-century America. Coming into adulthood during the 1950s and '60s, the cultural pieces were firmly in place which allowed a Caucasian man to climb the ladder of success with fewer barriers than most people face in our current time. Our family of five enjoyed a suburban home, vacations, and an upward mobility that was expected and encouraged by society. Toward the end of his working career my father indulged in frequent international travel. An annual winter condominium in Palm Springs and a cherry-red Porsche Carrera were badges of success – the fruition of the 'American Dream'.

After retiring from a career in engineering, my father found ways to serve others by offering his skills and expertise in service to his community. He participated in homebuilding projects with Habitat for Humanity, constructed an outdoor learning environment for local schoolchildren, and opened his home to international exchange students through the local Rotary Club. He enjoyed his few years as grandfather to my son and daughter and my sister's two children, my niece and nephew, who were all under the age of seven at the time of his death.

I traveled a lot during my twenties and often saw my family for just a few days a year before heading off somewhere else. My father carved out spaces for us to spend time together. We crossed the Cascade mountains on a day trip to the wineries of Eastern Washington where we picnicked on the grounds of green vineyards, enjoying the warmth of the sun on our cheeks as we sipped smooth Cabernet. On the ride back across the mountain pass we curved round steep bends as Rachmaninoff's Piano Concerto in D Minor played at volume on the car stereo. We spent a weekend driving down the Washington and Oregon coast, visiting sea lion caves and nibbling Tillamook cheese. Food, wine, and music became an integral combination of our shared times together. Just a week or so before his death, we sat together on the front porch, barefooted, sipping glasses of cool white wine and plucking out chords on our guitars. It is this final memory that I often cherish, that nourishes my own artist's soul and is the invisible, chimerical thread that binds me to the artist-side of my father.

The deep and resounding myth that arises from my work with this project is one of renewal. I choose to remember my father as a wide-eyed child picking wildflowers on a quiet country road, who is satiated by the song of a summer bird, and whose needs are simple and pure. A boy who created a "nest" out of a forgotten shed, danced around a homemade Maypole and watched in awed fascination as tendrils of smoke transformed into a raging forest fire. A boy who fished for eels with his grandfather, toes squishing through muddy riverbanks. I believe that returning to a simpler way of life, re-creating and re-imagining a humbler world, is not only appealing but necessary if we are to leave a living planet for those who come after us. May simplicity guide our hearts and hands as we turn back to nature, to wonder, to curiosity and creativity. To listen for the song of the nightingale before it is too late.

KIITOS!

Heartfelt gratitude extended to Sofia Rosales Makela for her original cover art and section illustrations; Jill Flores for interior and cover design; Piper Mertle for proof-reading; Jackie Brown for feedback on introduction and afterword; Nicole Winkler for edits on first and second drafts of complete work; Rachel Seick for final editing; Kat Dworkin for help with research and photographs; Village Books Independent Publishing Program; Finlandia Foundation National for the generous grant. And to Evelyn Makela, my mother.